TERRARIUM HABITATS

TEACHER'S GUIDE

Grades K–6

Skills
Observing, Comparing, Describing, Measuring,
Communicating, Organizing, Experimenting, Recording,
Drawing Conclusions, Building Models

Concepts
Soil and Ground Habitats, Ecology, Life Cycle, Food Webs,
Nutrient Cycle, Decomposition, Recycling, Adaptation,
Animal Structures and Behavior

Science Themes
Systems and Interactions, Patterns of Change, Structure,
Energy, Matter, Evolution

Mathematics Strands
Pattern, Number, Measurement

Nature of Science and Mathematics
Cooperative Efforts, Creativity and Constraints,
Interdisciplinary, Real-Life Applications

by
Kimi Hosoume with **Jacqueline Barber**

LHS GEMS

Great Explorations in Math and Science
Lawrence Hall of Science
University of California at Berkeley

Illustrations
Rose Craig

Photographs
Richard Hoyt

Cover Design
Lisa Klofkorn

Lawrence Hall of Science, University of California,
Berkeley, CA 94720

Chairman: Glenn T. Seaborg
Director: Marian C. Diamond

Publication of *Terrrarium Habitats* was made possible by a grant from the McDonnell Douglas Foundation and the McDonnell Douglas Employees Community Fund. The GEMS Project and the Lawrence Hall of Science greatly appreciate this support.

Initial support for the origination and publication of the GEMS series was provided by the A.W. Mellon Foundation and the Carnegie Corporation of New York. GEMS has also received support from the McDonnell-Douglas Foundation and the McDonnell-Douglas Employees Community Fund, the Hewlett Packard Company, and the people at Chevron USA. GEMS also gratefully acknowledges the contribution of word processing equipment from Apple Computer, Inc. This support does not imply responsibility for statements or views expressed in publications of the GEMS program. Under a grant from the National Science Foundation, GEMS Leader's Workshops have been held across the country. For further information on GEMS leadership opportunities, or to receive a publication brochure and the *GEMS Network News*, please contact GEMS at the address and phone number below.

International Standard Book Number: 0-912511-85-0

COMMENTS WELCOME

Great Explorations in Math and Science (GEMS) is an ongoing curriculum development project. GEMS guides are revised periodically, to incorporate teacher comments and new approaches. We welcome your criticisms, suggestions, helpful hints, and any anecdotes about your experience presenting GEMS activities. Your suggestions will be reviewed each time a GEMS guide is revised. Please send your comments to: GEMS Revisions, c/o Lawrence Hall of Science, University of California, Berkeley, CA 94720. The phone number is (510) 642-7771.

Great Explorations in Math and Science (GEMS) Program

The Lawrence Hall of Science (LHS) is a public science center on the University of California at Berkeley campus. LHS offers a full program of activities for the public, including workshops and classes, exhibits, films, lectures, and special events. LHS is also a center for teacher education and curriculum research and development.

Over the years, LHS staff have developed a multitude of activities, assembly programs, classes, and interactive exhibits. These programs have proven to be successful at the Hall and should be useful to schools, other science centers, museums, and community groups. A number of these guided-discovery activities have been published under the Great Explorations in Math and Science (GEMS) title, after an extensive refinement process that includes classroom testing of trial versions, modifications to ensure the use of easy-to-obtain materials, and carefully written and edited step-by-step instructions and background information to allow presentation by teachers without special background in mathematics or science.

Staff

Glenn T. Seaborg, **Principal Investigator**
Jacqueline Barber, **Director**
Kimi Hosoume, **Assistant Director**
Cary Sneider, **Curriculum Specialist**
Carolyn Willard, **GEMS Centers Coordinator**
Laura Tucker, **GEMS Workshop Coordinator**
Katharine Barrett, Kevin Beals, Ellen Blinderman, Beatrice Boffen, Gigi Dornfest, John Erickson, Jaine Kopp, Laura Lowell, Linda Lipner, Debra Sutter, Rebecca Tilley, **Staff Development Specialists**
Jan M. Goodman, Mathematics Consultant
Cynthia Eaton, **Administrative Coordinator**
Karen Milligan, **Distribution Coordinator**
Felicia Roston, **Shipping and Inventory**
Lisa Haderlie Baker, **Art Director**
Kay Fairwell, **Principal Publications Coordinator**
Carol Bevilacqua and Lisa Klofkorn, **Designers**
Lincoln Bergman, **Principal Editor**
Carl Babcock, **Senior Editor**
Staff Assistants: Erica De Cuir, Nancy Kedzierski, Vivian Tong, Leticia Valdez, Stephanie Van Meter, Mary Yang

Contributing Authors

Jacqueline Barber
Katharine Barrett
Kevin Beals
Lincoln Bergman
Celia Cuomo
Philip Gonsalves
Gigi Dornfest
Jaine Kopp
Linda Lipner
Laura Lowell
Linda De Lucchi

Jean Echols
Jan M. Goodman
Alan Gould
Kimi Hosoume
Susan Jagoda
Larry Malone
Cary I. Sneider
Debra Sutter
Jennifer Meux White
Carolyn Willard

Reviewers

We would like to thank the following educators who reviewed, tested, or coordinated the reviewing of this series of GEMS materials in manuscript and draft form. Their critical comments and recommendations, based on presentation of these activities nationwide, contributed significantly to these GEMS publications. Their participation in the review process does not necessarily imply endorsement of the GEMS program or responsibility for statement or views expressed. Their role in an invaluable one, and their feedback is carefully recorded and integrated as appropriate into the publications. THANK YOU!

ALASKA
Coordinator: Cynthia Dolmas Curran

Iditarod Elementary School, Wasilla
    Cynthia Dolmas Curran
    Jana DePriest
    Christina M. Jencks
    Abby Kellner-Rode
    Beverly McPeek

Sherrod Elementary School, Palmer
    Michael Curran
    R. G. Shenk
    Tom Hermon

CALIFORNIA
GEMS Center, Huntington Beach
Coordinator: Susan Spoeneman

College View School, Huntington Beach
    Kathy O'Steen
    Robin L. Rouse
    Karen Sandors
    Lisa McCarthy

John Eader School, Huntington Beach
    Jim Atteberry
    Ardis Bucy
    Virginia Ellenson

Issac Sowers Middle School,
Huntington Beach
    James E. Martin

San Francisco Bay Area
Coordinator: Cynthia Eaton

Bancroft Middle School, San Leandro
Catherine Heck
Barbara Kingsley
Michael Mandel
Stephen Rutherford

Edward M. Downer Elementary School, San Pablo
M. Antonieta Franco
Barbara Kelly
Linda Searls
Emily Teale Vogler

Malcolm X Intermediate School, Berkeley
Carole Chin
Denise B. Lebel
Rudolph Graham
DeEtte La Rue
Mahalia Ryba

Marie A. Murphy School, Richmond
Candice Cannon
Sally Freese
Dallas Karahalios
Susan Jane Kirsch
Sandra A. Petzoldt
Versa White

Marin Elementary School, Albany
Juline Aguilar
Chris Bowen
Lois B. Breault
Nancy Davidson
Sarah Del Grande
Marlene Keret
Juanita Rynerson
Maggie J. Shepard
Sonia Zulpo

Markham Elementary School, Oakland
Alvin Bettis
Eleanor Feuille
Sharon Kerr
Steven L. Norton
Patricia Harris Nunley
Kirsten Pihlaja
Ruth Quezada

Sierra School, El Cerrito
Laurie Chandler
Gary DeMoss
Tanya Grove
Roselyn Max
Norman Nemzer
Martha Salzman
Diane SImoneau
Marcia Williams

Sleepy Hollow Elementary School, Orinda
Lou Caputo
Marlene Fraser
Carolyn High
Janet Howard
Nancy Medbery
Kathy Mico-Smith
Anne H. Morton
Mary Welte

Walnut Heights Elementary School,
Walnut Creek
Christl Bluinenthal
Nora Davidson
Linda Ghysels
Julie A. Ginocchio
Sally J. Holcombe
Thomas F. MacLean
Elizabeth O'Brien
Gail F. Puleo

Willard Junior High School, Berkeley
Vana James
Linda Taylor-White

GEORGIA
Coordinator: Yonnie Carol Pope

Dodgen Middle School, Marietta
Linda W. Curtis
Joan B. Jackson
Marilyn Pope
Wanda Richardson

Mountain View Elementary School, Marietta
Cathy Howell
Diane Pine Miller
Janie E. Stokes
Elaine S. Toney

NEW YORK
Coordinator: Stanley J. Wegrzynowski

Dr. Charles R. Drew Science Magnet, Buffalo
Mary Jean Syrek
Renée C. Johnson
Ruth Kresser
Jane Wenner Metzger
Sharon Pikul

Lorraine Academy, Buffalo
Francine R. LoGrippo
Clintonia Graves
Albert Gurgol
Nancy B. Kryszczuk
Laura P. Parks

OREGON
Coordinator: Anne Kennedy

Myers Elementary School, Salem
Cheryl A. Ward
Carol Nivens
Kent C. Norris
Tami Socolofsky

Terrebonne Elementary School, Terrebonne
Francy Stillwell
Elizabeth M. Naidis
Carol Selle
Julie Wellette

Wallowa Elementary School, Wallowa
Sherry Carman
Jennifer K. Isley
Neil A. Miller
Warren J. Wilson

PENNSYVANIA
Coordinator: Greg Calvetti

Aliquippa Elementary School, Aliquippa
Karen Levitt
Lorraine McKinin
Ted Zeljak

Duquesne Elementary School, Duquesne
James Kamauf
Mike Vranesivic
Elizabeth West

Gateway Upper Elementary
School, Monroeville
Paul A. Bigos
Reed Douglas Hankinson
Barbara B. Messina
Barbara Platz
William Wilshire

Ramsey Elementary School, Monroeville
Faye Ward

WASHINGTON
Coordinator: David Kennedy

Blue Ridge Elementary School, Walla Walla
Peggy Harris Willcuts

Prospect Point School, Walla Walla
Alice R. MacDonald
Nancy Ann McCorkle

Acknowledgments

Special thanks to:

Katharine Barrett and Gigi Dornfest for their inspiration and support from start to finish—they helped develop the original classroom terrariums activity for the California State Department of Education's "Technology in the Curriculum" science resource guide project in 1984. See the "Resources" section of this guide for a bibliographical listing.

Jean Echols and other PEACHES staff members who continued to refine aspects of these activities for the PEACHES Homes in the Ground early childhood guide. PEACHES stands for Preschool Explorations for Adults, Children, and Educators in Science. PEACHES is an early childhood science and mathematics program based at the Lawrence Hall of Science.

Carole Chin's fourth grade class at Malcolm X school in Berkeley, who enthusiastically built terrariums, watched seeds grow, and excitedly observed the behavior of isopods and crickets. Some of their journal entries and drawings appear in this guide.

All my friends and colleagues who share my fondness for small creatures...those who brought in precious garden soil, backyard snails, pillbugs, sowbugs, plants, and many other ideal terrarium residents for my office and indoor habitats everywhere.

Jacqueline Barber and Lincoln Bergman for their invaluable help in pulling the guide together, thereby helping this GEMS guide bring out the excitement, wonder, simplicity, and beauty of the living world of a terrarium habitat.

 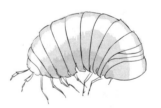

The GEMS Project and the Lawrence Hall of Science would particularly like to thank Steve Van Zandt and the world-famous Banana Slug String Band for allowing us to reprint the words and music for two great songs, "Dirt Made My Lunch" and "Decomposition." These songs are © 1979 by Steve Van Zandt, and are used here with his gracious permission. For more information about the Banana Slug String Band, relating to performances, tapes, and songbooks, please contact the Banana Slug String Band, P.O. Box 2262, Santa Cruz, CA 95063. Many other Banana Slug String Band songs relate well to this *Terrarium Habitats* unit, as well as to other GEMS activities, such as *Animals in Action*, *Earthworms*, *River Cutters*, and *Tree Homes*.

Contents

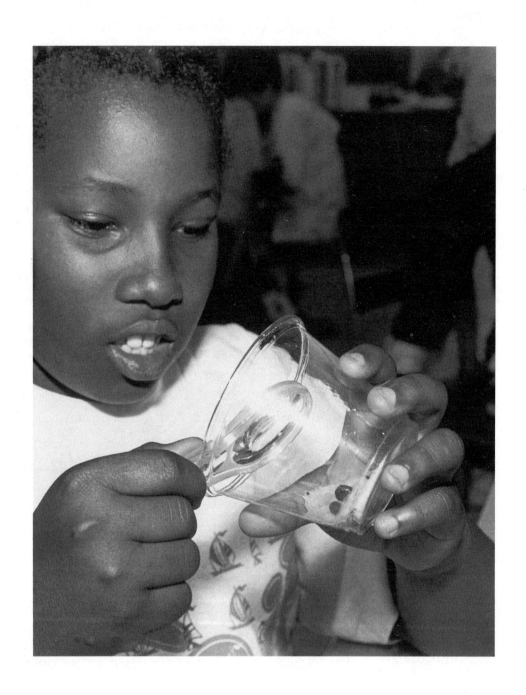

Introducing Terrarium Habitats

A different world—of earthworms and insects, seeds and plant roots, tunnels and burrows—exists beneath the surface of the ground. This underground habitat supports tiny plants, animals, and bacteria called decomposers. Decomposers, such as earthworms, pillbugs, and fungi, recycle the nutrients in once-living things and return them to the soil. The cycle begins again when plant roots take up these nutrients for the growth of new leaves and stems. These plants eventually become food for other animals.

This process of decomposition takes place continuously in the soil without most of us noticing or understanding its significance. Since all animals, including humans, depend on plants for the basis of our food supply, the natural recycling process going on beneath our feet is of tremendous importance. Squeeze some garden soil through your fingers and smell its earthy smell after a warm spring day. Observe a tiny sprout push through the ground. This series of activities gives students firsthand experiences with the work of the tiny soil inhabitants!

You may be lucky enough to have a garden or forest floor nearby for your class to investigate. Still, bringing soil indoors and creating a living terrarium provides a vital laboratory for observing nature's processes. There are opportunities for students of every age to learn from terrariums! Students of different levels will approach a terrarium in different ways. As their teacher, you can provide older students with increasingly more sophisticated challenges. This is one activity that can be done each year with more and different benefits!

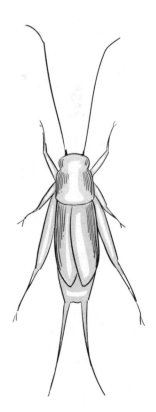

In *Activity 1: Exploring Soil,* your students have an opportunity to focus on observing soil. Most students are quite intrigued by and interested in examining soil, especially when they find out that soils come in different colors, textures, odors, and contain tiny familiar living things. Yes, soil is much more than dirt, and even your students who have an initial aversion to getting dirty will want to touch and explore! An optional simple test in a vial with soil, water, and alum separates the soil into distinct layers, allowing your students to actually see the composition of soil.

A *habitat* must include everything a plant or animal needs to survive. In *Activity 2: Building a Terrarium Habitat,* your students work together to build their mini-forest habitat in a plastic container using soil and a variety of natural items like leaves, bark, bird seed, and strawberry plants.

Easily obtained animals like earthworms and pillbugs are first observed carefully and then placed into the terrariums in *Activities 3 and 4.* Continuing to observe the terrarium is the most exciting part of the activity. Did the isopods have babies? What happened to the dried leaves? Where did these white eggs come from? Look what sprouted from the seeds! Student journals of observations and drawings record the daily changes. Students enjoy observing the animals' behaviors and interactions with the terrarium. Many of the animals will reproduce in the terrarium. Plants and food items will decompose. Your students will see, firsthand, the role the animals play in the process of decomposition. Although decay is a process that some people avoid and some students can react to because dead things smell when they break down and look strange, too. But for all of its unpleasant aspects, organic decomposition is essential to the well-being of life on earth. The nutrients within once-living things are digested by scavengers and decomposers and, through their waste, returned back to the soil.

Older students may map the movements of the creatures in the terrariums. They can also plan and carry out their own more controlled investigations and/or do further research for a term or group project. Of course, observing and caring for the terrariums is an ongoing activity that will involve your students for as little or as much time as you choose.

Activity 5: Adding More to the Terrarium provides your students with the opportunity to explore interactions within their terrarium habitats as they choose and add other animals, plants, food items, and/or objects of their choice. This open-ended activity can last for weeks or even months, as students sharpen their observation skills and increase their understanding of the interactions within their own group's terrarium.

The "Behind the Scenes" section contains information on maintaining terrariums. Unlike most animal habitats, terrariums take very little maintenance! The main problems occur when terrariums are over-watered. Don't worry if the lush patch of grass turns yellow and begins to rot—this is part of the natural cycle of plants that will unfold as your students watch. Also, don't be surprised if a snail eats all foliage in sight! Providing enough supplementary food, adding more seeds and plants and/or removing one or more animals can stimulate new growth and new interactions to observe. These terrariums habitats are ever-changing—observe and enjoy the changes and see if you and your students can cause some changes of your own.

Summary Outlines are provided to help you guide your students through these activities. Additional, removable copies of student data sheets are included at the end of the book for your copying convenience.

Most of the materials for *Terrarium Habitats* come from outdoors or the grocery store. Enlist the help of your students to bring in soil, worms, snails, seeds, or leftovers from lunch! Then find some plastic containers and let students loose to design their microhabitats. For perhaps the rest of the school year, your students will be continually amazed with the world of living soil in a terrarium habitat!

Time Frame

Note: The best time to conduct these activities is during the spring and early fall when garden animals, plants, and good soil are abundant and accessible. Cold weather and hot, dry climates drive snails, pillbugs, and earthworms underground or to more protected areas in your garden.

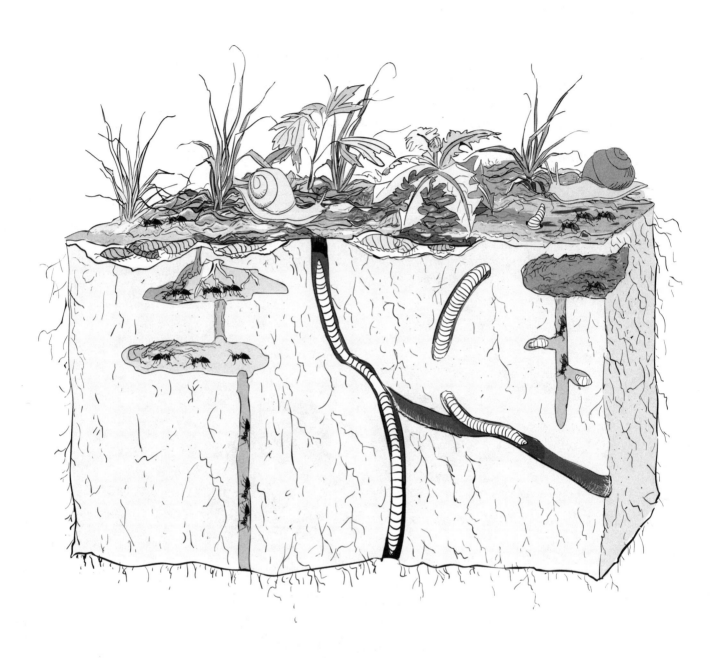

Activity 1: Exploring Soil

Soil is beneath our feet every day, but we seldom get a chance to examine it closely. In this activity, students work in teams of four to carefully observe and describe a sample of garden or backyard soil. They observe the color, texture, and odor of the soil and use magnifying lenses to examine things in the soil such as roots, leaves, earthworms, and pebbles. Following investigations of the soil, a class discussion enables students to share their findings and to learn about soil's relationship to other living things. They learn that soil is not "dirt," but instead is a living "coat" on the earth.

The activities in this session encourage students to: sharpen their observation and communication skills as they make careful observations of soil; discover that soil contains living and non-living things including water and the nutrients necessary for life; understand soil's place in the ecosystem as it relates to plants, animals, and humans; and change negative attitudes about soil as dirty, "yucky," or not worthy of study.

Teachers of older students for whom some of the above-mentioned objectives are already familiar might want to consider having their students investigate and compare more than one kind of soil. This will focus them on fine observations, comparisons, and an understanding that not all soils are the same. If you decide to do this we recommend choosing two very different soils, such as potting soil and backyard soil; a clay soil and a sandy soil; or rich garden soil and trampled playground soil. You will need to adjust the preparation for the session accordingly.

An optional soil profile test for older students is described on pages 11–12. Background information is included in the "Behind the Scenes" section on page 59. This simple test enables students to separate the different components of soil into layers, and to compare their relative amounts, thereby making visible and concrete a collection of otherwise abstract concepts. If you decide to do this test with your students, either as a hands-on activity or as a demonstration, plan to do it in another session.

What You Need

For the whole class:
❏ 2 water misters
❏ 2 sponges

For each team of four students:
❏ 1 cup of garden soil
❏ 1 or 2 plastic sandwich bags (to contain soil)
❏ 4 pieces of white scratch paper (to use as soil observation mats)
❏ 4 pencils
❏ 2 magnifying lenses
❏ 4 plastic spoons
❏ newspapers
❏ 4 journals or blank booklets for recording observations throughout the unit
❏ Optional: 1 tray for organizing team materials

Getting Ready

A Week Before the Activity

1. Collect some clean garden soil or have students bring in a sandwich bag filled with soil from home. Choosing a sample of soil from the school or a nearby area is usually of high interest to students. Store the soil in a cool, non-sunny place in the classroom.

2. Sometime before the activity, lightly mist the soil if it is dry. This will reduce dust and enhance the natural odors of the soil. Divide the soil samples into plastic sandwich bags, one for each group.

3. Collect the rest of the materials needed for this activity.

4. Read the "Behind the Scenes" information on soil.

The Day of the Activity

Set up two materials distribution stations from which the students can obtain their materials. Organize the materials into groups for each team.

Immediately Before the Activity

Place newspapers out on the tables or have sponges available for clean-up.

Introducing the Activity

1. Tell students they will be investigating a very important natural resource that supports plant and animal life on our planet—soil. As a group, make two lists: First ask, "Where have you found soil?" Write all responses on the board. Then ask, "What do you think we will find in the soils?" Record all predictions.

2. Tell the students that now they will have a chance to test their predictions of what's in soil, by carefully observing everything they can about soil. Show the bags of soil and tell where they came from. Tell the students that they will make observations of the soil using four of their five senses. "Which senses will you use to observe the soils?" Sense of sight, hearing, touch, and smell are fine to use, but tell them they will not be tasting the soil.

Be sure to see the song "Dirt Made My Lunch," featured, with music, on page 49 of this guide.

3. Tell the students that when they get their materials each person should place one spoonful of the soil onto her white paper, observe it, and write or draw descriptions on the paper. Even though each student has his own soil sample, explain it's okay for groups to explore and discuss the soil together.

Investigating the Soil

1. When students understand what they are to do, have one student from each group come up and get the soil along with spoons, white paper, magnifying lenses, and pencils for the group.

2. Circulate among the different teams to encourage their investigations. Suggest other ways to observe the soil such as misting it with one squirt of water and smelling it, squeezing some between their fingers, rolling it into a ball, smearing the damp soil on the paper to note the color, or using the magnifying lens.

3. Younger students will naturally make many observations of the soil but may need help articulating what they have observed. Some older students may curtail their observations because it's "just dirt." You may need to challenge them to come up with at least three observations with each sense—that makes a total of twelve! Ask students who have an easy time making multiple observations to notice with which sense it's easiest to make observations and with which sense it's more difficult.

4. Encourage the students to share their observations with the other team members.

Reflecting: Soil is More than Dirt!

1. After at least five minutes of observation, have students share and discuss their findings. Write their descriptions on the board next to their list of predictions about what's in soil. Compare their predictions to their observations. Ask, "What was something unexpected that you found out about your soil?

2. Have your students help you draw a simple food chain, beginning with the plants and the successive animals that depend on the plants for food, by asking them questions and then drawing their responses. For example, you might ask, "What eats rabbits? [See diagram on page 13.]

3. As it becomes clear how soil relates to humans, lead a short discussion on the importance of soil for plants, animals, and human survival. As they observed, soil contains living and non-living things, water and nutrients necessary for life. Conclude by emphasizing how soil is much more than stuff that gets you dirty! Without soil, all life on our planet is threatened!

4. For older students, describe how soil is like a living coat that covers the surface of the planet. Today, there is a worldwide problem of soil destruction. In the United States alone, thousands of acres of agricultural soil are destroyed each day as soil is covered with roads and buildings, contaminated with chemicals, or eroded due to deforestation or overgrazing by cattle and sheep. New soil can take hundreds or thousands of years to develop, depending on the climate and the plants and animals living in the soil. Desert areas of the world are increasing, in part due to soil erosion caused by human activities.

5. Have the students put their spoonfuls of soil back into the bags. As the groups finish, have them begin cleaning up. Spoons and hand lenses can be rinsed. Clean newspaper can be saved for the next activity with tables sponged off if needed. Students should wash their hands after handling the soil.

Going Further (for Activity 1)

1. Bring in several different soil samples and have your students observe and compare their properties. Do they have the same color? texture? odor? moisture content? For older students: Have your students conduct and compare soil profile tests of each of these soils.

2. For older students: To capture small soil animals, set up a funnel full of soil to capture the small mites, springtails, worms, and isopods that live in soil. Put a small amount of steel wool (must not contain cleansers) in the bottom of a large funnel to keep the soil from falling through the hole. Gently place 1–2 cupfuls of rich garden soil in the funnel. Balance the funnel in a glass jar or clear cup that contains about an inch of water. Place a desk lamp with an incandescent bulb above the funnel (with the bulb about 8 inches from the soil). The tiny animals will move downward through the soil to escape the heat, and will fall into the water. Use spoons and magnifying lenses to capture and examine the animals.

The optional Soil Profile Test described on page 11 allows students to "see" the components of soil for themselves and to compare how much of each component is present in a particular soil sample. While doing this test requires you to gather another set of materials and to dedicate another class session, teachers have found it to be an extremely worth-while and rewarding activity, especially with older students.

— Fresh Soil

— Steel Wool

— Water

3. Bring in a variety of uprooted plants so that the students can observe root structures with magnifying lenses.

4. Take the class outside to look at a roadside cut through a bank of soil or show drawings and photos of a cutaway view of a forest floor. Have students collaborate to make a mural of a cross-section of soil showing animal burrows, tree roots, leaf litter, dark layer of humus, developing soil, and rocky subsoil. Students can add drawings of organisms to appropriate areas of the mural.

5. Have your students make pictures by rubbing and smearing different colored soils on white paper. You and they will be amazed by pictures created with these natural earth pigments!

Modifications for K-2

1. Take the students on a walk to observe and collect soils or have them bring in soils from home.

2. Place the soil in paper lunch bags and introduce them as "feely" bags. (If soil is very damp it may break through the paper bags.) Encourage students to feel the soil, describe what it feels like, and compare it to the contents of other bags. Follow the "feely" bag introduction with the observation of soil on paper.

3. Either don't use magnifying lenses or use this activity as an opportunity to introduce magnifying lenses and their proper use. Let students freely explore with the magnifying lens and then show them how to magnify objects. Begin with their fingertips, a page from a book, or cloth from their sleeve. Have them place the lens on top of the object and then slowly move the lens toward their eye. They should see the object magnified at about 1–2 inches from the surface of the object.

4. Conduct the soil observation activities in small groups with an adult supervising the materials, leading the discussions, and facilitating the simple investigation.

5. Keep the objectives of the activity limited to observing and describing soil and then, how soil helps plants and animals (provides food, water, air, a place to live, warmth, protection).

6. Limit the length of whole group discussions and list-making on the board.

Soil Profile Test (Optional)
(recommended for 4th–6th grade students)

Soil scientists observe soil with their senses, but they also do tests with the soil to learn more about it. The test described here enables students to observe the different components of soil. Have students work in teams using plastic vials to conduct and observe their own soil profile tests or do a class demonstration using one or more large glass jars.

What You Need

For each team of four students:
- ❏ 4 clear plastic vials with lids (approximately 1" in diameter, 3" high)
- ❏ 4 plastic spoons
- ❏ 1–2 tablespoons of alum (available from a well-stocked grocery store)
- ❏ 1 cup or plastic sandwich bag to contain alum
- ❏ 1 measuring cup containing 1 cup of water
- ❏ newspapers

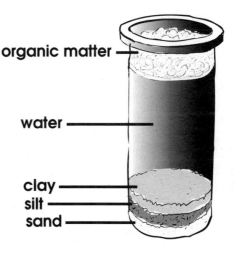

organic matter

water

clay
silt
sand

soil + alum + water

What You Do

1. Mark the lid of a clear plastic vial with the type of soil you are testing.

2. Fill the vial with approximately one inch of soil.

3. Add a large pinch of alum (exact quantities do not matter). Tell the students that the alum is a chemical that is used in making pickles. It won't hurt them to touch it, but they shouldn't put it in their mouths. The alum acts as a dispersing agent, helping the soil particles to break into smaller parts and settle out into layers by weight.

4. Fill the vial to the top with water; cover, shake vigorously, and then let stand. **It is important not to move the vial once it has been shaken and placed on the table.**

5. After several minutes, have everyone observe and record the soil profile. While they are waiting, encourage your students to make predictions of what they will see when the contents of the vial settle.

6. After everyone has drawn, ask, "What happened after you let your test sample settle? How many layers did you get? What are they like?" You may want to ask, "What do you think is at the bottom of the profile? Why is it at the bottom? What is at the top of the water? Why is it floating on top? What do these layers tell us about the soil?" [some layers are heavier than others, some layers are larger, and **for older students:** the layers show *how much of each component* is in the soil.]

7. Most soils have two or three layers on the bottom and a small layer floating on top of the water (see diagram on previous page). You may want to introduce the terms used by soil scientists to describe each layer: the floating layer is the *organic matter,* the top layer is *clay,* the middle layer is *silt,* and the bottom layer is *sand.*

8. Ask," Which layer is the largest? the smallest? Is any layer missing?" Clay soils are characterized by being sticky or tacky when wet. They can easily be rolled into a ball and absorb and retain water. Sandy soils are more crumbly and drain water rather than retain it. Ask students if their observations of the soil and its properties are verified by what they discovered about the soil through the soil profile test.

9. It's fascinating to set the soil profiles on a shelf or windowsill and continue to observe them later that day, the next day, or even several days later. If they are left undisturbed, the layers should become even more pronounced.

You may want to have students conduct and compare soil profile tests of different soils by looking for similarities and differences. A common difference they will find is different amounts of organic matter. Lead a discussion about why some soils had more organic matter than others. [There weren't many plants that died, gardeners may have added organic matter or compost.] If students don't bring up *compost,* introduce it as vegetable and other plant matter that is left to rot. When it has broken down a bit, it can be added to the garden soil to provide nutrients for the plants.

Clean-up: Soil profiles in the vials can be saved for future observations. (The soil particles in the water will continue to settle out and algae may grow.) Vials can also be dumped into a central bucket or tub. Again, let the soil settle out and the remaining water can be poured down the sink. The soil can be rinsed again to remove the alum. **(Do not use this soil in the terrariums.** Rinsed soil can be safely recycled onto landscaped areas or flower gardens.)

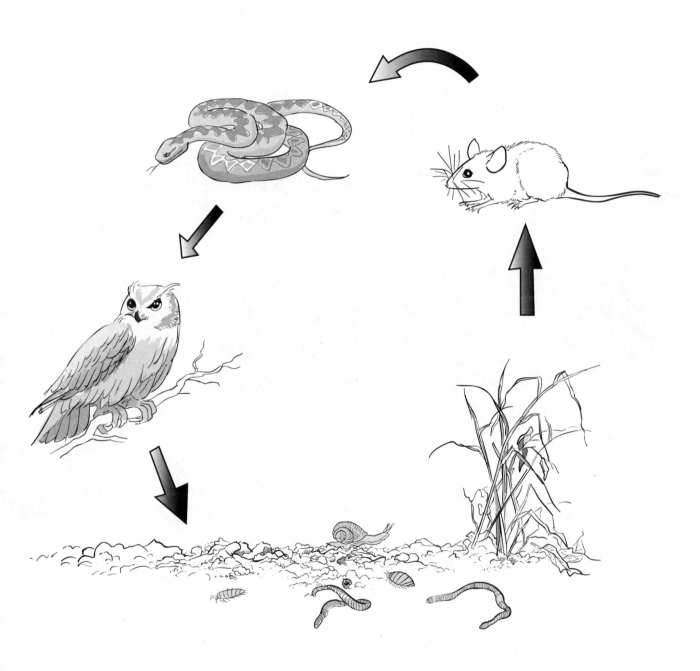

Activity 2: Building a Terrarium Habitat

In this activity, each team of four students builds a terrarium in a plastic container by first putting in a layer of soil and then adding plants, seeds, leaves, twigs and water to create a habitat for ground-dwelling animals.

Teams discuss the necessary requirements for an animal's home or habitat and think of animals that could live in their terrarium successfully. The terrariums are placed in areas with adequate warmth and light. Students decide on a schedule for observing. Recordings are made in a journal, and include both written and pictorial observations.

The activities in this session encourage students to: work cooperatively in teams as they design and build their "world in a box" and help them develop an understanding of the concept of a habitat.

What You Need
(For each team of four students)
Note: If you would like to make a demonstration terrarium, plan as if you had one extra team.

- ❏ 1 small, clear plastic storage box with lid, or a clear plastic salad container
- ❏ 1 push pin for making holes in terrarium lids
- ❏ enough soil to fill 1/3 of the container when mixed with sand
- ❏ sand equal to 1/4 the amount of soil
- ❏ 1 teaspoon of birdseed or grass seed
- ❏ 1 handful of dry leaves from fruit, oak, birch, maple or leaves from other deciduous trees
- ❏ 1 small plant such as strawberry, sweet alyssum, violets, or other small garden plants
- ❏ 1–2 twigs or pieces of bark
- ❏ 2–3 plastic spoons for mixing soil
- ❏ 1 spray bottle for water
- ❏ 1 piece of black construction paper large enough to cover one side of the box
- ❏ 1 white self-adhesive label or strip of masking tape to stick on piece of black construction paper
- ❏ 1 roll of transparent tape for attaching black paper to terrariums
- ❏ 4 journals or blank booklets for recording observations throughout the unit

Getting Ready

Several Days Before the Activity

Pieces of cardboard tubing make interesting animal hideouts that will naturally decompose.

1. Read the "Behind the Scenes" section beginning on page 59 to learn more about the handling and maintaining of the soil, plants, and animals you will be adding to the terrarium.

2. Gather the materials needed to present the activity. Caution: Be aware that soils may contain molds, fungi, parasites, and chemicals that can cause health problems for people. Collect soil only from clean areas, away from pets, and wash your hands after handling the soil.

3. Punch six to ten small holes into the lids of the terrarium containers for airflow. Push-pin holes are the easiest to make in thin plastic. Small air holes may have to be drilled into thicker plastic containers.

4. Attach a white label of strip of masking tape to one side of each piece of construction paper.

The Day of the Activity

1. Set up two materials distribution stations from which the students can obtain their supplies. Organize the materials into groups for each team.

2. Lightly mist the soil if it is dry. This will reduce dust, enhance the natural odors, and reduce the chance of students inhaling or ingesting dust.

Immediately Before the Activity

Place newspapers out on the tables or have sponges available for clean-up.

We put the s and in the teerrariuhi. And we mix the soil. We put the water.

What's In A Terrarium?

1. Ask the students to think of the ground or floor beneath a forest. "What might you find on the forest floor?" Hold up the various materials you have gathered as students mention them (soil, sand, leaves, seeds, fruit, plants, water, twigs, or dry grass). Tell the students that these are some of the things they will put in a container to make a home for living things.

2. Now is the time to demonstrate the making of a terrarium (if you have planned to do that) or for explaining the various components of a terrarium so your students can plan their own. Show the plastic container, spoons, and water sprayers that the teams will be using and explain each of the following parts of a terrarium either as you demonstrate the building of yours, or as you provide verbally step-by-step information to assist their planning.

Adding soil. Depending on the level of your students and the number of variables you would like to offer, there are two choices regarding soil: **a) how much** (not to exceed 1/3 the volume of the container; and **b) its composition** (optimum is approximately 1 part sand to 4 parts soil). If you want to remove all choice, pre-mix the sand and soil and instruct the students to fill the container approximately 1/3 full with soil mix. Complete choice would involve students in deciding how much soil they think is needed to support the plants and animals that will live in the terrarium, and how much sand they should add to their soil mix (reminding them that sand increases drainage). Students may also decide **c) the landscape of the soil** in their terrarium, for instance whether they'd like to make a flat landscape or one with hills and valleys.

Planting plants. Describe how to make a hole in the soil, loosen the plant from its container, carefully place the roots and soil of the plant in the hole, add soil, and firmly press the surface of the soil on all sides of the plant's stem. Your students may choose **a) where they plant their plant.** Depending on how many plants you have collected and of what variety, your students may also be able to choose **b) how many plants** to have in their terrariums and **c) what kind.**

Introduce the word terrarium by comparing it to the word aquarium. An aquarium is a place for living things that live in water, a terrarium is a place for living things that live on land [terra=land, aqua=water].

Spreading seeds. Show the seeds that you have collected—bird seed and/or grass seed. Explain that they may decide **a) what kind(s) of seeds to plant** (if you have more than one kind), **b) how much** (you may want to place an upper limit), and **c) where** (evenly in the whole terrarium? in one area?). Once they decide, sprinkling the seeds on the surface of the soil is adequate. There is no need to cover them with soil, unless students would like to see the difference between covered and uncovered seeds.

Adding litter (twigs, bark, and leaves). Show the leaves and twigs you have collected. Students may choose: **a) whether to add leaves and twigs, b) how much to add, and c) where to put them.**

Adding moisture. This should be done twice: once after the soil is added and then again as the last thing that is done in building the terrarium. Show them the mister. Remind the students that they are not building a swamp or a pond! In fact, too much moisture can be a problem in a terrarium. **Limit the number of squirts to four per student; two to moisten the soil and two to add to the completed terrarium.**

3. Some teachers, especially those of older students, like to provide roles for each of the students. One possible arrangement could be: Soil Mixer, Soil Adder, Planter, Seed Spreader and Leaf and Twig Adder. Then all students can share in adding moisture. Other teachers, especially those of younger students, like to dole out tasks (and materials) one at a time and encourage their students to share in the doing of those tasks. Plan how you'd like to structure the terrarium building and if you plan to have different roles for each student, assign them now.

4. Have teams begin discussing their plans *before* the materials are distributed. You may want to provide older students with paper to sketch their plans. Some teachers have had students make their planning sketches in their journals.

Building the Terrariums

1. As the groups complete their planning, have one or two students from each team come up and get the materials for building a terrarium.

2. Circulate and encourage the teams to be cooperative in creating the terrarium. Remind them to mist the soil, the plants, and the seeds lightly, and have them use spoons to mix the soil mixture in the container.

3. Give the teams a chance to view the other terrariums and to share techniques, discoveries, and aesthetics of their design.

Introducing the Concept of Habitat

1. Gather the students together for a discussion. "Why did we add plants? [for food, shelter,)] leaves? seeds? twigs?" The terrarium you have can also be called a *habitat*. "What is a habitat?" [A place where animals live, like a neighborhood.] "What does a habitat need to provide?" [food, shelter, moisture, light, protection—all the things an animal needs to live and survive.] Each terrarium is like a miniature world in a box, containing all of the things that the plants and animals in that world will need.

2. Ask, "What kinds of animals might live in this habitat?" [salamanders, pillbugs, snails, worms, crickets, slugs] Tell the students that they will be adding animals to their terrarium and then observing what happens over time in future sessions.

Older students may enjoy doing a soil profile test on their soil mixture and recording the profile on a sheet of paper. Doing a second test on the terrarium soil after six weeks may show a surprising change. If you decide to do this, have vials, lids, water, and alum available.

Caring for and Observing the Terrariums over Time

1. "What kinds of changes will we see in our terrariums?" [plants will grow, seeds will sprout, dead leaves will rot, mold will grow] Discuss the following procedures for terrarium maintenance:

- Decide on a place for the terrariums to reside. Choose places that get some natural light, but no direct sunlight. A cool place is much better than a spot next to the heater.

- Decide on a schedule for watering. If the terrarium is fairly damp, two squirts of water **per week** are fine. Adjust the watering if your room is warm or if swamps were created on the first day. Terrariums smaller than a shoe box will need very little water to stay moist. *Note:* Too much water will cause many problems in a terrarium. When in doubt, **less is better.**

- Lids stay on the terrariums unless someone is making careful observations which require an up-close view. All leaves and twigs must be carefully placed back in their original positions.

- Terrariums should not be bumped or shaken.

2. Plan a routine for observing the terrarium and keeping a record of changes. Older students can keep a journal of writing and drawings or team members could take turns observing the terrarium throughout the day, noting the date and time of day. Younger students can draw pictures, dictate observations, or share their observations verbally on a daily basis.

We put soil.
And sand leaves.
And a plant.
It was brown and black

Providing a Dark Place in the Habitat

1. Show the teams the black papers with labels. Have everyone sign the team's label to identify the terrariums. Teams may like to name their terrarium. Demonstrate how to tape the top edge of the paper to the outside of one side of the terrarium to form a flap. The paper will create a "dark side" of the terrarium where animals may congregate. Lifting the flap will reveal animal hiding places above and below the surface of the soil.

2. Have teams make and attach the label flap, move the terrariums to their spots, and clean up their work tables. Students should wash their hands after handling the soil and other materials.

Modifications for K-2

1. Go on a walk to collect leaves, twigs, seeds, plants for the terrarium or send lunch bags home to have parents and children help with the collecting.

2. Create mystery "feely" bags with the soil, seed, twigs, and leaves, and make observations on each before placing them in the terrarium.

3. Make one classroom terrarium together as a demonstration with students coming up to plant seeds, mix soil, add leaves, etc.

4. Have adult volunteers supervise the making of the small group terrariums after the demonstration terrarium is made.

5. Stress the concept of the terrarium as a **home for plants and animals.**

Activity 3: Adding Earthworms to the Terrarium

Students are excited about their terrariums and will immediately want to add small insects, worms, and other things! In this activity, students observe the structure and behavior of earthworms and then place them in their terrariums. Students are introduced to the concept of adaptation as they speculate on why the earthworm looks and behaves as it does. Students are also introduced to the concept of decomposition and of the earthworm's role as a "decomposer." If you haven't already done "worm" activities with your students, be prepared for a treat! It's surprising how engaged and fascinated students become as they observe earthworms.

The activities in this session encourage students to: gain a first-hand understanding of earthworm structures and behavior; adopt a positive attitude about earthworms and their value; learn about the important concepts of adaptation and decomposition; understand the role earthworms play in the ecosystem.

What You Need

For the whole class:
- ❑ 2 water misters
- ❑ 1 tray or piece of cardboard for sorting earthworms
- ❑ 1 push pin for making holes in lids of worm containers
- ❑ Optional: 2 sponges or newspaper to cover tables

For each pair of students:
- ❑ 2 earthworms (redworms or bait worms)
- ❑ 1 half-gallon milk carton tray or other small tray with sides (see Getting Ready for how to make milk carton trays)
- ❑ 2 clear plastic cups
- ❑ 2 pencils
- ❑ 1 magnifying lens
- ❑ 1 or 2 damp dried leaves or moist 2" x 2" paper towel pieces
- ❑ 2 journals or blank booklets for recording observations throughout the unit
- ❑ Optional: 2 earthworm student sheets for older students (master on page 31)
- ❑ Optional: 1 plastic spoon
- ❑ Optional: 1 small plastic ruler
- ❑ Optional: 1 nightcrawler earthworm

Getting Ready

A Week Before the Day of the Activity

1. Read the "Behind the Scenes" section on earthworms.

2. Collect earthworms from gardens, purchase redworms from bait stores, or have students bring in earthworms from home. Earthworms can be transported easily and kept in a plastic container with a lid containing moistened soil or peat moss. The container should only be half full of soil. Tiny pin holes in the lid, along with the air space in the container, will allow for enough air circulation. Store the worms in a very cool place in the room or in the warmer part of a refrigerator for up to a week. Check on the worms to make sure they and their surroundings are **moist.**

3. Duplicate one copy of the earthworm student sheet for each student if you plan to use it. (Master on page 31.) Teachers of the very youngest and the very oldest students sometimes prefer using a more open-ended recording format. Older students can be asked to draw the structure of their worms and describe its behavior.

4. Gather the rest of the materials needed for the activity.

5. Make a milk carton tray for each pair of students by cutting a half gallon milk carton in half lengthwise. Staple the spout closed so both halves may be used. (See diagram on this page.) Milk carton trays can be rinsed out, dried, and used in future activities.

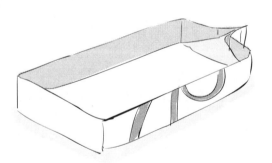

Immediately Before the Activity

1. Pour out the earthworms onto a tray. Redworms usually clump together in a cluster or ball. Mist lightly to remove the soil around them and place one worm in a cup for each student. Mist the worms again. Place another tray over the cups if you will not be handing out the worms in the next 10 minutes. As the worms warm up they will begin to move out of the cups!

2. Set up two materials distribution stations from which the students can obtain their supplies.

3. Have terrariums nearby but not in the team work areas. This will encourage the students to observe their earthworms before putting them into the terrariums.

Observing Earthworms!

1. Tell your students that today they will put some living animals into their terrariums. Ask, "What small animals spend most of their time underground?" [moles, ants, earthworms] Tell them that today the earthworm will be the animal they will be observing closely.

2. Ask, "What do you know about earthworms? Where do you see them? What were they doing?" Encourage the students to tell about their experiences with earthworms.

3. Some students are likely to bring up the fact that worms are "disgusting" or "icky" or they just don't like them. This is a great opportunity to say that they will be observing earthworms today to learn more about them and especially to learn what is positive and interesting about worms. Reassure students that they don't have to touch the worms, but they do have to treat them gently.

4. Hold up a worm in a clear plastic cup and show how to hold the cup up to the light and see the internal structures of the worm. If they like, students can use the magnifying lens and spoon to move and observe the worm gently. Show the student sheet, and invite the students to draw an outline of the worm with any internal or external structures that they observe.

5. After they have observed the worms in the cup they can place a worm into a milk carton tray to observe its movements. One or two damp dried leaves can be added to the tray to see how the earthworms respond to them.

6. Have one person from each team come up and get the materials for their team.

7. Circulate among the teams to help them in their observations and recording. Take along the mister to lightly mist any worms that are drying out. Encourage gentle and quiet handling of the earthworms. Worms are quite resilient. As long as they are kept moist and not submerged in water they will be very interesting and active!

Biological supply houses such as Ward's, NASCO, and Carolina Biological sell earthworms. (As noted in the Resources section, these suppliers also sell isopods, snails, and other organisms, as well as plants, containers, etc.).

Chemicals (enzymes) in the earthworm's gut break down decayed plants in the soil as food for the worm. But what comes out as waste (castings) has been changed so that remaining nutrients are now available for plants to use. Along with soil, earthworms will eat dead leaves and other plant material from the top of the ground. They pull dead leaves down into their tunnel and while doing so, mix the soil with nutrients. The tunneling creates spaces for air and water for plants, and homes for other animals. Earthworms not only produce rich soil, they prepare it for other plants and animals to use!

8. This may be the first time some of your students have handled or examined an earthworm closely. They will be very excited, so circulate and focus their excitement with questions and suggestions. Challenge your students to find the head [the pointed end], the tail, and determine the worms' reaction to touch, light, darkness, moisture, dryness. Ask, "What can you see inside?" [dark tube - intestine, and red tubes - blood vessels] "What does a worm feel like?" [slimy, bumpy]

9. Encourage the students to fill-in a drawing of a worm and to write down or draw their observations of the worms' movements and reactions to other things.

10. **Optional:** Older students can be asked to attempt to measure the length and diameter of their worms. This can involve some estimation depending on how cooperative the worms are. If there is variation in the size of the worms you have this data can be fun to graph.

11. **Optional:** If you have obtained nightcrawlers, have one student from each pair come up with an empty cup and get one to observe. Students can compare this larger worm with their redworm and record their observations on another outline of an earthworm.

12. **Optional:** Older students may want to conduct some of the experiments mentioned in the book *Earthworms, Dirt and Rotten Leaves*. (See "Going Further" on page 29.)

What Did You Find Out?

1. Before the wrap-up discussion, direct the students to place the worms back in the cups and put a damp leaf on top to encourage the worm to stay in the cup.

2. Have one team member return the milk carton trays, the lenses, and spoons. Draw a large outline of the earthworm on the board.

3. Have all of the students turn their attention to the front of the room. Ask, "What is something you discovered about your earthworm?" Lead a discussion on their earthworm observations, inviting students to come up and add structures or labels to the worm outline. You or volunteers can begin a list on the board of their observations.

4. As students bring up earthworm characteristics, ask them to speculate about the benefit of the structures or behaviors to the survival of the worm in an underground home. For younger students, ask, "How does being slimy (or long or cylindrical) help an earthworm to move (or burrow)? Write their answers in a separate column next to the list of characteristics.

5. After the lists have been added to and discussed, introduce the concept of *adaptation*. Tell the students that the structures or behaviors that help an animal to survive are called adaptations. Adaptations make an animal better adapted or suited for life in their particular environment. Ask, "What are some human adaptations that help us to survive?" [The structure of our hands, arms, legs, feet for grasping, climbing, pulling, pushing, walking and running; our developed sense of taste, hearing, touch, smell, sight.]

6. Tell the students that an earthworm's adaptations also benefit the soil and in turn, plants that grow in the soil. Ask, "What do earthworms eat?" [From the appearance of their intestine, they seem to eat soil!] Explain how earthworms act as "recyclers" by eating dead plants that are in the soil and breaking them down so the nutrients that were in the plants are now in the soil again, ready to be absorbed by a new plant's roots. Introduce the word *decomposition*. Teachers of older students may want to name this as a *nutrient cycle*.

Adding Earthworms to the Terrariums

1. By now, everyone is ready to put their earthworms in the terrariums. First, have them predict what the earthworm will do when it is placed inside.

2. Have the original terrarium team get together and send one team member to bring the terrarium to the table. One at a time, they can carefully place their worm and leaf into the terrarium. All team members should observe what each earthworm does. Older students can directly record the earthworm behavior in a journal or on the student data sheet.

3. Each team should clean off their table, rinse out cups, trays, spoons and set them aside to dry. Students should wash their hands after handling earthworms and soil.

More on Earthworms

Once the earthworms are added to the terrariums, they will spend most of their time underground. This in and of itself is a telling observation about earthworm behavior! However students are often anxious to see the earthworms again. Here are a couple of tips for helping them do so:

1) Earthworms come out at night. Ask your students to think of a way to simulate nighttime and "fool" the earthworms into coming to the surface. (They might decide to leave a terrarium in a dark closet, or enclose it in a larger dark box or paper grocery bag.)

2) Careful observation on the sides of the terrarium often reveals earthworm tunnels and glimpses of the worms. Look especially under the black flap on the side of the terrarium.

3) Look for evidence of earthworms, such as a pile of castings (dirt formed in squiggle-like piles) at the top of worm tunnels. Gently moving the castings aside will often reveal the tunnel, which will satisfy some students!

Most of all, instruct your students to be patient and extra-observant. Some animals are elusive! If several earthworms were added to the terrarium, it is likely that they will reproduce, which may increase the likelihood that they'll see one. Many students have delighted to see the young earthworms. It's possible—keep trying!

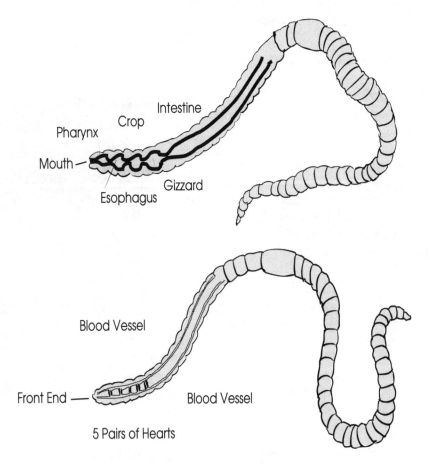

Going Further

1. Encourage students to collect redworms and nightcrawlers at home from their yards, beneath flower pots, or from the sidewalks after a rain. More observations and simple experiments can be conducted in the classroom and the worms added to the terrariums or returned outdoors.

2. Have the book, *Earthworms, Dirt and Rotten Leaves* available for 4th–6th graders to read (and for teachers to read, too!) It is an easy-to-read book that discusses everything-you-need-to-know-about-earthworms and their contributions to soil ecology. The simple experiments make a nice individual or team project for those students curious about earthworm behavior.

3. Students can write stories about life underground from an earthworm's perspective. Letters from an "earthworm" to a "cousin earthworm" can be written describing how they escaped being eaten by a bird or being washed away by a heavy rainstorm.

4. Have students research and build a "worm bin" to observe the decomposition of organic material by worms and the production of soil. A worm bin is a box containing soil, vegetable material, and earthworms. Students may be familiar with a similar box called a compost bin. Contact a local ecology or gardening center for more information on worm and compost bins. See "Composting Across the Curriculum" and other materials listed in the "Resources" section on page 53.

5. Try "the old worm and shovel trick" with your students to observe how earthworms respond to vibrations. See pages 62–63 of "Behind the Scenes" for a description of how to use a vibrating shovel to get earthworms to crawl to the surface of a lawn.

6. Consider presenting one or more of other related GEMS activities, depending on grade level and your desired curricular emphases. Among GEMS guides that make a strong connection with the Terrariums unit are: *Earthworms; Animals in Action; Mapping Animal Movements;* and *Mapping Fish Habitats.*

K-2 Modifications

1. Go on a walk to collect worms for the terrarium. Compare the size, color, and shape of the worms. Observe where you find the worms and what makes a good earthworm home.

2. Young children love to handle earthworms. Encourage them to moisten their hands with water and to handle the worms gently. Children's hands should be rinsed of soap or lotions before touching earthworms to prevent injury to the worms.

3. Have students do more hands-on investigation of the earthworms with more guided discussion by the teacher or a small group adult leader.

4. Do less recording on the board, and have students draw their earthworms in context, rather than adding to an earthworm outline. Say, "Draw a picture of your earthworm living in your terrarium or in a flower garden." You probably won't want to use the student sheet that is provided.

5. Keep a daily watch and group log on the terrarium for earthworm burrows, or castings or leaves that disappear.

6. Young students do not need to be introduced to the words adaptation or decomposition, but the basic concepts, explained simply, are very appropriate for them to learn.

1. It looks like a jungle.

2. We see a stick.

3. It has ants.

4. We see roots.

Observing Earthworms

1. Draw what your earthworm looks like:

Inside View:

Outside View:

2. What does your earthworm do?

Activity 4: Adding Isopods to the Terrarium

Rolly-pollys, pillbugs, sowbugs, potato bugs—these are all names for the tiny isopods that are commonly found under flowerpots and logs. During their childhood, most students have collected them from their gardens or sidewalks. They are harmless, active, and fun to observe!

In this activity your students observe behavior to identify the differences and similarities between pillbugs and sowbugs. Placed in the terrariums, the isopods will burrow in the soil, hide under leaves, and munch away at the food provided.

The activities in this session encourage students to: identify and understand isopod structures and behavior; adopt a positive attitude about isopods and their value; learn about the important concept of adaptation; understand the role pillbugs and sowbugs play in the ecology of the soil.

There are two kinds of isopods. Those that roll into a ball are commonly called "pillbugs" or "rolly-pollys." They have a rounded shape, smooth edges, and no spines in the rear. "Sowbugs" are the common name for the isopod that cannot roll into a ball—its shell is flat with fringed edges and it has two spines out the back. Isopods are also called "wood lice," "pill wood lice," or "potato bugs" by some people.

What You Need

For the whole class:
- ❏ 2 water misters
- ❏ 1 push pin for making holes in lids of isopod containers
- ❏ Optional: 2 sponges or newspaper to cover tables

For each pair of students:
- ❏ 4 isopods: 2 sowbugs and 2 pillbugs (See Getting Ready for where to get isopods.)
- ❏ 1 half-gallon milk carton tray or other small tray with sides (see Getting Ready for how to make milk carton trays)
- ❏ 1 clear plastic cup with lid
- ❏ 2 pencils
- ❏ 1 chunk of raw potato at least the size of a large marble
- ❏ 2" x 2" damp paper towel or 2 damp dried leaves of about the same size
- ❏ 1/4 of a cardboard tube from a roll of toilet paper
- ❏ 2 journals or blank booklets for recording observations throughout the unit

❏ Optional: 2 isopod student sheets for older
    students (master on page 41)
❏ Optional: 1 plastic spoon
❏ Optional: 1 small plastic ruler

Getting Ready

A Week Before the Activity

1. Read the "Behind the Scenes" section on isopods.

2. Collect pillbugs (rolly-pollys) and sowbugs from gardens
or have students bring in isopods from home. Look under
flower pots, along edges of lawns, under leaf litter and rocks.
Pillbugs prefer drier areas around sidewalks and bricks
while sowbugs prefer damp, protected spots near vegetation.
Isopods can be transported easily and kept in a plastic
container with a lid containing damp dried leaves or paper
towels. Tiny pin holes in the lid, along with the airspace in
the container, will allow for enough air circulation. Store the
isopods in a very cool place in the room for up to a week. It
is very important to keep the isopods on moist paper or
leaves at all times.

3. Duplicate one copy of the isopod student sheet for each
student if you plan to use it. (Master on page41.) Teachers
of the very youngest and the very oldest students sometimes
prefer using a more open-ended recording format. Older
students can be asked to draw the structure of their isopods
and describe their behavior.

4. Gather the rest of the materials needed for the activity.

5. Make a milk carton tray for each pair of students by
cutting a half gallon milk carton in half lengthwise. Staple
the spout closed so both halves may be used. (See drawing
on this page.) Milk carton trays can rinsed out, dried, and
used in future activities.

The Day of the Activity

    Set up two materials distribution stations from which
the students can obtain their supplies.

Biological supply houses such as Ward's, NASCO, and Carolina Biological sell isopods. (As noted in the Resources section, these suppliers also sell earthworms, snails, and other organisms, as well as plants, containers, etc.).

As with the earthworms, it's more exciting to keep the identity of the animals a secret. But if you've had students help you collect them, then describe them generically as "those rolly polly or potato bug type animals." Through investigation, the students will be discovering that there are two distinct types of isopods that they are observing.

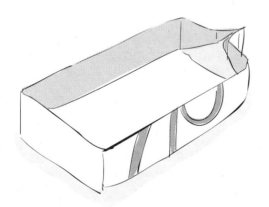

Immediately Before the Activity

1. Place leaves or paper towels into each cup. Mist lightly to dampen them and place two pillbugs and two sowbugs into a cup. Mist the isopods again and place a tight lid on each cup.

2. Have terrariums nearby but not in the team work areas. This will encourage the students to observe their isopods before putting them into the terrariums.

Observing Isopods!

1. Tell your students that they are ready to observe another living animal that could live in their terrarium. Ask, "What small animals have you seen under leaves or logs on the ground?" [ants, earthworms, beetles, rolly pollys] Introduce the animals in the cup as isopods, a Latin word for "same or identical-looking legs."

2. Have a student look at a cup closely and tell the class the more common names for isopods. Ask, "What do you know about isopods? Where do you see them? What were they doing?" Encourage the students to tell about their experiences with pillbugs and sowbugs.

3. Some student is likely to express an opinion that isopods are "scary" or "icky" or that "they just don't like" them. This is a great opportunity to say that students will be observing them today to learn more about them and especially to learn what is positive and interesting about isopods. Reassure students that they don't have to touch the isopods, but they do have to treat them gently.

4. Hold up a cup of isopods and show how you can look from below and see the underside structures of the animals. If they like, they can use the magnifying lens and spoon to observe the isopods gently. Show the student sheet. The students are to draw a side view, top and bottom view of the isopods.

Isopods are included in the larger group of animals called crustaceans. Most crustaceans are found in the sea, such as lobsters and shrimp. They are characterized by having segmented body parts, appendages, and a hard shell. Isopods are terrestrial crustaceans that are found in damp areas to prevent water loss from their body.

Pillbug

5. After they have observed the isopods in the cup they can place them into a milk carton tray to observe their movements. The damp dried leaves, a paper towel, potato chunk, and piece of cardboard tube can be added to the tray to see how the isopods respond to them.

6. Have one person from each team come up and get the materials for their team.

7. Circulate among the teams to help them in their observations and recording. Take along the mister to lightly mist any isopods that are drying out. **Encourage gentle and quiet handling of the isopods.** Isopods are very active!

8. This may be the first time some of your students have handled or examined an isopod closely. They will be very excited, so circulate and focus their excitement with questions and suggestions. Challenge your students to find the antennae, head, eyes, the number of legs, segments, and determine the isopods' reaction to touch, light, darkness, moisture, dryness. Ask, "How do the isopods behave?" or "What do the isopods do? What does an isopod feel like?" [hard, smooth].

9. Encourage the students to make drawings of the isopods and to write down or draw their observations of the isopods' movements and reactions to other things.

10. **Optional:** Older students can be asked to measure the length and width of their isopods.

What Did You Find Out?

1. Before the wrap-up discussion, direct the students to place the isopods back in the cups with a damp leaf and put the lid on.

2. Have all of the students turn their attention to the front of the room. Ask, "What is something you discovered about your isopods?" Lead a discussion on their isopod observations, inviting students to come up and draw and label a picture of an isopod. You or volunteers can begin a list of their observations on the board.

3. Ask questions to bring out the different characteristics of isopods, both physical and behavioral. Do not tell them they have two kinds of isopods, rather, let them discover this through their own discussion and observations. "What kinds of body shapes did you observe?" [flat, round, oval]

"Did they have antennae?" [Yes, and some have spine-like structures extending from the rear.] "How did they move or what did they do?" [moved fast, slow, rolled into a ball]

4. During the discussion, students will have differing opinions and discover that not all of the isopods share the same characteristics. If someone does not point out that there are two kinds, then ask, "Are all of the isopods the same?" [No, although there are many shared characteristics— segmentation, number of legs, smoothness, hardness, size— there are distinct characteristics belonging to the two types of isopods.]

5. Go through the list and have students pick out the characteristics that belong to the ones that roll into a ball. [pillbugs have a rounded shape, smooth edges, no spines out the rear.] These isopods are probably the most familiar to youngsters. Tell them that one general name for them is "pillbug" because they roll into a ball or pill. Have students pick out the characteristics of the other type of isopod [sowbugs are flat with fringed edges and have two spines out the back. They cannot roll into a ball.] Another common name for sowbugs is wood louse because they are found beneath damp wood. Students may be more familiar with the name sowbug.

6. As students bring up isopod characteristics, ask them to speculate on the benefit of the structures or behaviors to the survival of isopods in a ground home. For younger students, ask, "How does being dark in color help an isopod?" [Helps to "hide" it or camouflage it against the dark ground] Write their answers in a separate column next to the list of characteristics.

7. After the lists have been added to and discussed, review the concept of *adaptation* as those structures and behaviors that help an animal to survive in its environment.

8. It is interesting to compare the adaptations for defense of the pillbug and sowbug. Set the scene by saying, "A hungry bird spies a pillbug and a sowbug on the ground. What could the isopods do to defend themselves from the bird?" [Pillbugs can curl up into a ball, protecting their soft underside, or roll away or blend in with the environment like a small pebble. Sowbugs can scurry under a rock or plant or log, or lie very flat and still to blend in with the environment.]

Chemicals (enzymes) in the isopod's digestive tract break down decayed or rotten material as food. But what comes out as waste (or frasse) has been changed so that remaining nutrients are now available for plants to use. Isopods do some burrowing like earthworms, mixing the soil, providing spaces for water and air. But their biggest contribution to the soil is helping in the decomposition of dead plants and animals. The waste products of isopods are in fact rich soil particles, full of nutrients for plants!

9. Tell the students that an isopod's adaptations benefit the soil and, in turn, benefit the plants that grow in the soil. Ask, "What do isopods eat?" The students may have noticed munched leaves or potato or the tiny dark square specks of waste (frasse) on the paper towels or trays. Isopods are scavengers that eat dead plants and animals. Like earthworms, isopods act as recyclers or decomposers as they break down former plants and animals into nutrients that new plants need to grow. Re-emphasize the importance of decomposition in the ecosystem of a forest floor (and everywhere!).

Adding Isopods to the Terrariums

1. By now, everyone is ready to put their isopods in the terrariums. First, have them predict what the pillbugs and sowbugs will do when they are placed inside. Will they behave differently?

2. Have the original terrarium team get together and send one team member to bring the terrarium to the table. One at a time, they can carefully place their isopods, leaves, potato chunk, and cardboard roll into the terrarium. All team members should observe what each isopod does. Older students can directly record the isopods' behavior in a journal or on the student data sheet.

3. Each team should clean off their table, rinse out the cups, trays, spoons and set them aside to dry. Students should wash their hands after handling the isopods and soil.

Going Further

1. Conduct isopod races. First, make a circle with string, chalk or marker on construction paper, about the size of a medium pizza. Place a pillbug and a sowbug in the center— the first one to reach the edge of the circle wins! Repeat the races and keep track of which ones win. Make some predictions. Do more pillbugs or sowbugs win the races? How do their movements help them to survive? Large paper plates make good race tracks, too!

2. Encourage students to collect isopods at home from their yards, beneath flower pots, or from under bushes. Challenge the students to discover if sowbugs and pillbugs live in different types of places (sowbugs prefer a damper environment, while pillbugs prefer a drier one). More observations and simple experiments can be conducted in the classroom and the isopods added to the terrariums or returned outdoors.

3. Have the book, *Earthworms, Dirt and Rotten Leaves* available for 4th–6th graders to read. Isopods are also a part of an earthworm's habitat and some of the experiments can be conducted with isopods instead of earthworms. The experiments make a nice individual or team project for those students curious about isopod behavior.

4. Students can write stories about life above and below ground from an isopod's perspective. Letters from a pillbug to sowbug or from a sowbug to a pillbug can be written describing, for example, how they escaped from being eaten by a bird.

5. Several other GEMS guides feature activities that can be related to these terrarium activities. In the GEMS *Earthworms* guide, students experiment with changes in earthworm pulse rates related to temperature. Other guides for upper elementary students include *Animals in Action, Mapping Animal Movements,* and *Mapping Fish Habitats.* Related GEMS guides for preschool and the early elementary grades include *Ladybugs* and *Tree Homes.*

Sowbug

K-2 Modifications

1. Go on a walk to collect isopods for the terrarium. Compare the size, color, and shape of the isopods. Observe where you find them and discuss what makes a good isopod home.

2. Have students do more hands-on investigation of the isopods with more guided discussion by the teacher or a small group adult leader. Create an isopod obstacle course in the trays using leaves, twigs, potatoes. What do they do?

3. Do less recording on the board, and have students draw their isopods in context. Say, "Draw a picture of your isopod living in your terrarium or in a flower garden." You probably will not want to use the student sheet that is provided.

4. Keep a daily watch and group log on the terrarium for isopod burrows, waste, or leaves and potatoes with munch marks.

Name_____

Observing Isopods

1. Draw what your isopods look like:

Side View:

Top View:

Bottom View:

2. What do your isopods do?

Activity 5: Adding More to the Terrarium

This section includes ideas for ways to introduce other things to your students' terrariums. The "Behind the Scenes" section has other possibilities, too. Use these suggestions as a springboard for your own ideas!

Some teachers have let each student team choose one thing per week to add to their terrarium and then the group observes what happens. In this way, different groups added different things and made unique discoveries that they were anxious to share with the rest of the class. This method also generated ongoing excitement as each group discussed and planned what they would add next. Student-led investigations are often the most powerful!! The terrarium lid is the limit!

Your students may become disappointed as they watch the plants and animals in their terrariums undergo the natural life cycles of life, death, and decomposition. Help them understand that this is part of a larger cycle. Also, see the information about maintaining terrariums in the "Behind the Scenes" section, beginning on page 59, for ideas of how to keep the terrariums living and how to re-start some of these cycles.

What You Need

❑ small animals collected by students such as: garden snails, slugs, beetles, garden crickets, garden spiders, millipedes, etc.
❑ food items brought in by students such as: potato, carrot, apple, corn, eggshells, lettuce, dried beans
❑ inanimate objects brought in by students such as: rocks, shells, sand more dried twigs, wood, leaves, plants (even weeds), bird and grass seed.
❑ time for your students to observe and describe (orally or in their journals) their new discoveries!!

See the sample letter on page 57. Consider using it or a letter like it to enlist the help of parents in obtaining items that can be added to the terrariums.

What You Don't Need!!!

✘ small animals such as poisonous spiders and centipedes. Flying animals such as adult butterflies, flies, moths, ladybugs or the same animals in their younger life stages like caterpillars. (Most of these animals require a specific kind of food that won't be available in the terrarium.) Ants will not live long and may invite an ant trail linking your terrariums to other parts of the classroom.

✘ food items such as candy, bananas, tomatoes, and other soft fruits that will encourage an unwanted population of flies or ants. Also, stay away from broccoli, other cabbages, and meats that may have a strong odor as they decompose.

✘ small plastic toys: your students will want to add them to the terrarium scene. It's up to you. You could limit the amount so it doesn't become a "Disneyland!"

Once established, your students' terrariums can be habitats for a variety of small animals! Encourage students to bring in other animals for their terrariums such as **garden snails, slugs, beetles, garden crickets, garden spiders, millipedes.** All of these animals can be safely collected from home gardens and yards, with the supervision of an adult. **Brown crickets** can be purchased from pet stores and are interesting animals to observe and add to the terrarium. Vertebrate animals such as small **salamanders, tree frogs, and toads** will be able to visit terrariums for a week or so. They will eat the young isopods, mites, and spiders that live beneath the leaves. Encourage the students to find out the requirements of these larger animals; this may lead to creating a larger terrarium habitat and providing other foods for them to eat. Vertebrates collected from outdoors should be returned to the wild if students are unable to care for them adequately.

There are lots of other non-animal things that can be added to a terrarium that result in interesting interactions. A piece of **carrot, apple,** or **celery** will serve as both food and shelter for some of the small animals. Watching it be eaten, lived in, and decompose can be very interesting. A piece of **corn on the cob** (uncooked) may also serve a variety of functions. It may even sprout!! **Egg shells** will provide calcium for the isopods. The dark pieces of isopod waste left on the white egg shells are interesting clues to the identity of the nighttime forager! Invite your students to judiciously add scraps from their own lunches and see what happens. Students sometimes enjoy seeing how animals interact with certain kinds of objects as well. A favorite **rock or shell, peach or avocado pits,** and even a small pile of **sand** can be interesting to add.

Getting Ready

1. Read the sections on **"Snail Observations"** and **"Cricket Observations"** on the following pages, as well as information in the **"Behind the Scenes"** section on other animals you're considering adding to the terrariums.

2. Decide what you'd like your students to add to their terrariums.

3. Plan how you will gather the additional things to add to the terrariums, and begin collecting. them You may want to enlist the help of your students and their parents. Duplicate or modify the sample letter on page 57 if you intend to involve parents in collecting items.

4. Decide how you want to structure the activity of students adding more to the terrariums. For example, will you choose what to add and when, or will the students choose what to add and when, etc. There are many ways to proceed and you probably have your own ideas and preferences. One good sequence that many teachers have suggested is the following: Week #1: Add snails; Week #2: Add crickets; Week #3 (and after): Team's choice of what to add.

5. As desired, prepare or have students create observation sheets for the organisms to be added. Consider assigning journal or other writing activities for students to describe the changes they observe in their terrariums over time.

Interactions Abound

1. Depending on the options and approach you've decided upon, explain to your students that they will now be adding other organisms and materials to their terrariums.

2. If snails are among the organisms being added, have your students make snail observations and, if desired, conduct the other activities described under "Snail Observations" on page 46. Please consider the cautionary note regarding adding only one or two snails to any one terrarium!

3. If crickets are among the organisms being added, have students do the cricket observation activities described under "Cricket Observations" on page 47 and, if desired, the obstacle race challenges as well.

4. Over the next several weeks, encourage students to record their findings, ask questions, test their assumptions, and in general learn more about the inhabitants and interactions within their "world in a box."

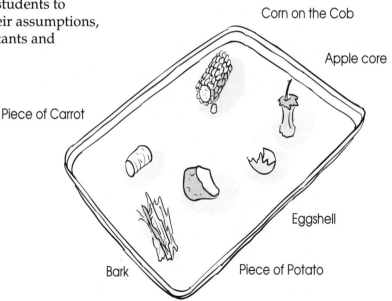

Corn on the Cob

Apple core

Piece of Carrot

Eggshell

Bark

Piece of Potato

Snail Observations

Garden snails from your yards are excellent animals to observe and care for in the terrariums. Students can safely collect them after it rains or after the garden is watered. See the "Behind the Scenes" section on page 66 for more information about snails.

1. Have each student observe their own snail in a clear cup. Encourage them to look for structures and behaviors. Three especially interesting ones are:

> a. The contraction of the muscles that can be observed in the foot (visible with a clear cup). Students should see a wave-like motion as the snail moves across the clear surface.

> b. If offered a piece of lettuce, most snails will eat, showing their mouth-part called a radula. If the head of the snail is light in color, students may see the lettuce moving down the intestine!

> c. Snails have four feelers with eyes positioned on top of the top two feelers. Explore what happens when you lightly touch the eyes! (If done gently, it does not harm the snail.)

2. Set up an obstacle course on tables using cups, rulers, branches, different fabrics, different foods, wire, string, and observe how the snails move through the course.

3. Conduct snail races on the same circular isopod racetracks, as described in the "Going Further" section for Activity 4. The surface of the track should be smooth, like a desk top, clear plastic sheet, or paper plate.

4. Have students design experiments to see if snails have food preferences, or color preferences. How strong are snails? How much weight can they hold with their foot? How much weight can they pull?

5. Collect slugs, and compare their structures and behaviors to snails.

6. Record observations, draw pictures, and discuss physical and behavioral adaptations of the snail. Place one or two small snails into each terrarium. Snails can be sparingly marked with nail polish or "white-out" on their shell and their movements mapped over time.

Don't add more than one or two snails to each terrarium. They will eat most plants in sight! While this is interesting (and natural!) students sometimes grieve the deforestation of their terrariums! One alternative is to continually replant and/or provide supplementary greens for the snails to eat. Another is to plant something like ivy or marigolds, plants which snails don't prefer. You could also have students remove the snails after several weeks of observing them in the terrarium. It's fine to keep the snails in the terrarium, but it will change the terrain. An advantage to having two snails is the opportunity of watching the snails mate, lay eggs, and seeing 20 or more tiny snails emerge. You might want to designate one terrarium as a snail habitat.

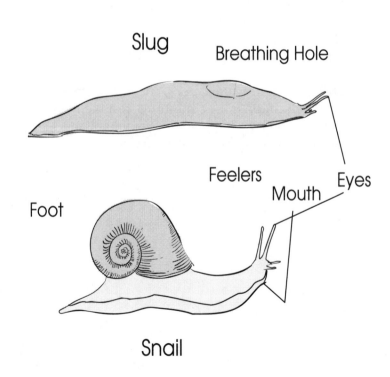

Cricket Observations

Brown crickets are safe to handle and fun to watch. Your students will enjoy their chirping in the terrariums. Most pet stores sell them as food for other animals. See the "Behind the Scenes" section on page 65 for more information about crickets.

1. Place a male and a female cricket in each cup with a damp paper towel and lid. Provide one cup for every two students. Have the students observe the crickets. Encourage them to look for structures and behaviors. Challenge them to identify the male and female. The students will notice the ovipositor on one cricket, but will assume that it is the male!

2. Set up an obstacle course or a maze in a deep cardboard box using cups, rulers, branches, different fabrics, different foods, wire, string, and observe how the crickets move through the course. They can still crawl out of the box, but slow hand movements and interesting things to investigate should keep them inside for a while. If they do get out, move slowly and gently cup your hand around them.

3. Record observations, draw pictures, and discuss physical and behavioral adaptations of the cricket. Place two to four crickets into each terrarium. Crickets prefer it on the drier side of damp. Add dry cardboard tube or egg carton houses for the crickets to hide in and to keep them dry. Keep one side of the terrarium dry especially for the crickets. Students may see their crickets reproduce. Keep a piece of apple or carrot or a piece of dry dog or rat food in the terrarium for food.

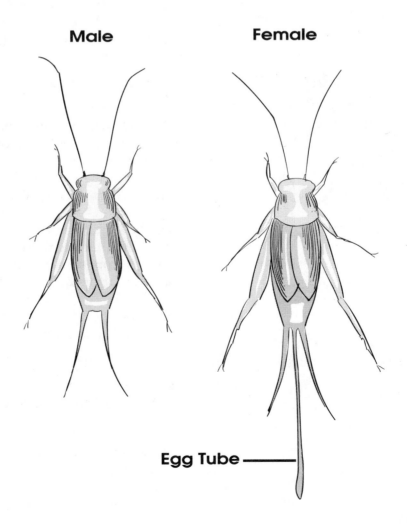

Male   **Female**

Egg Tube ————

Going Further

1. Older students can draw a map of their terrarium and observe and record the daily changes in all parts of the terrarium. Do certain animals cluster by the potato? in drier areas? in wetter areas? What foods do they prefer?

2. A simple population study for older students would be to keep track of the number of earthworms, isopods, crickets and snails in the terrarium. All of these animals can reproduce in the terrariums. For an accurate count, the terrarium can be carefully taken apart to find the animals underground.

Your students may enjoy the "Decomposition" song on page 50.

3. Have your students make decomposition bags. This activity enables your students to compare the process of decomposition as it happens in the terrarium (with the help of the decomposers, earthworms and isopods!) with decomposition of food in plastic bags. Older students will appreciate the similarities and differences between the two situations. ALL students will appreciate the opportunity to touch and feel the decomposing material as it lets off heat and undergoes a dramatic change of texture.

MAKE DECOMPOSITION BAGS!

a. Put an identical amount and selection of foods in two different ziplock bags. (Foods such as fruits, vegetables, breads, pasta, and seeds are ideal. Avoid meat, eggs, cheeses, oily things, and smelly vegetables like cabbage that produce strong odors when they decay.)

b. Then change one thing about one of the bags. For instance you could put one bag in the dark and one in the light; one bag could have holes in it (exposed to air) and one could be sealed; one bag could have moisture added and one bag left dry; or one bag could have earthworms in it and the other could have no worms.

c. By comparing the rate of decomposition in the two bags, your students can draw conclusions about the factors that facilitate decomposition.

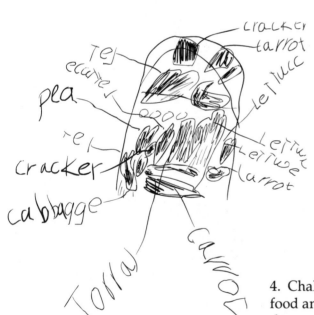

4. Challenge each student to make their own sketch of a food and energy cycle that includes people as well as decomposers.

5. Have students write a science fiction story about what life on earth might be like if all of the decomposers became extinct.

6. Have students bring in some products that are advertised as "biodegradable," and set up experiments to see whether or not they decay.

Dirt Made My Lunch

by Steve Van Zandt

Chorus:
Dirt made my lunch, dirt made my lunch.
Thank you dirt, thanks a bunch
For my salad, my sandwich, my milk, my munch.
Dirt made my lunch.

Dirt is a word we often use
When we talk about the earth beneath our shoes.
It's a place where plants can sink their toes
And in a little while a garden grows.

Chorus

A farmer's plow will tickle the ground.
You know the earth has laughed when wheat is found.
The grain is taken and flour is ground
For makin' a sandwich to munch down.

Chorus

A stubby green beard grows upon the land.
Out of the soil the grass will stand
But under hoof it must bow
For makin' milk by way of cow.

Chorus

Decomposition

© 1979 by Steve Van Zandt. Used with permission.

There are many kinds of bugs,
Worms and snails and banana slugs.
They are useful for me and you,
They help to make the soil renew.
Well come all you people gather round, break down, and listen to...
CHORUS

Decomposition is a useful game.
A tree drops its leaves but they don't stay the same.
A bug chews them up and spits them back out
Making the soil for a new tree to sprout.
Well come all you people gather round, break down, and listen to...
CHORUS

Resources

Ordering Live Animals

Alameda County Home Composting
7977 Capwell Drive
Oakland, CA 94621
Rotline: (510) 635-6275
Earthworms and other live creatures
plus educational books and materials.
No isopods. Call for brochure.

Bassett Cricket Ranch
535 North Lover's Lane
Visalia, CA 93291   (209) 732-2738

Carolina Biological Supply Company
2700 York Road
Burlington, NC 27215 (919) 584-0381

Connecticut Valley Biological Supply Co.
82 Valley Road P.O. Box 326
Southampton, MA 01073 (800) 638-7748

Delta Education, Inc.
P.O. Box 915
Hudson, NH 03051-0915 (800) 258-1302

Fisher Scientific Company
4901 W. Lemoyne Street
Chicago, IL 60651 1 (800) 621-4769

Insect Lore
P.O. Box 1535
Shafter, CA 93263
1-800-LIVE BUG
Earthworms and other live creatures plus educational
books and materials. No isopods. Call for brochure.

McKilligan Supply Corporation
435 Main Street
Johnson City, NY 13790 (607) 729-6511

Nasco
901 Janesville Avenue
Fort Atkinson, WI (800) 558-9595

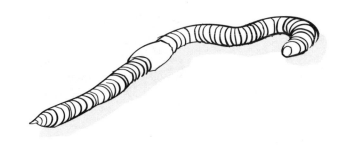

Nasco West, Inc.
P.O. Box 3837
Modesto, CA 95352 (209) 545-1600
(earthworms and crickets; no isopods)
Rainbow Mealworms, Inc.
P.O. Box 4907
Compton, CA 90224
1-800-777-9676
(310) 635-1494
FAX (310) 635-1004
Note: Mealworms and crickets only available through mail.
Redworms and nightcrawlers available at the store.
Call for brochure.

Science Kit and Boreal Labs
777 E. Park Drive
Tonawanda, NY 14150 (800) 828-7777

Ward's Natural Science Establishment
P.O. Box 92912
Rochester, NY 14692-9012 (800) 962-2660

Western Scientific Company
P.O. Box 681
West Sacramento, CA 95691   (916) 371-2705

I learned About the krikits wer leapeing ololet.

I found out that Eerth wruMs Git log

I Wundr if I poct the krikit sreits it Woodd
I mit Bea wut

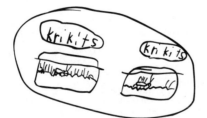

Helpful Books and Other Resources

The Amazing Dirt Book: Two dozen fun projects for home or school by Paulette Bourgeois, Addison-Wesley Publishing Company, Inc., New York, 1990. Extremely accessible, concise and cleverly written book that intersperses numerous short features and answers to intriguing questions abput dirt in all its apects, with science activities. Part of Chapter 4 on "Dirt Homes," relates directly to *Terrarium Habitats.*

Compost! A Teacher's Guide to Activities & Resources in the East Bay by Cindy Nelson, Sarah Shaffer, and Cindy Havstad, and published by the Alameda County Home Composting Program (address and phone number listed above). This is an excellent series of activities on composting and recycling, with well-summarized information and an excellent listing of related resources.

Composting Across the Curriculum: a Teacher's Guide to Composting by Marin County Office of Waste Management. An outstanding collection of activities for preschool through adult. This guide contains a 26 clearly-written lessons plus instruction on how to compost, vocabulary, background information for teachers and designs for building your own compost or worm bin. Cost is $ 8.50 per copy. To order, or for more information, contact: County of Marin, Department of Public Works, Office of Waste Management, P.O. Box 4186, San Rafael, California, 94913, (415) 499-6647.

The Compost Heap by Harlow Rockwell, Doubleday and Company, Inc., 1974. For very young children.

Creatures in the Classroom, Multnomah County Education Service District, Portland, Oregon, 1976. This comprehensive resource book is available from: Curriculum Department, Multnomah County, Education Service District, P.O. Box 16657, Portland, OR 97216, (503) 255-1841.

Earth Science for Every Kid by Janice Pratt VanCleave, John Wiley & Sons, New York, 1991. 101 hands-on investigations.

Earthworms, Dirt, and Rotten Leaves: An Exploration in Ecology by Molly McLaughlin, illustrated by Robert Shetterly, Avon Publishing, New York, 1986. An excellent, clearly-written and illustrated book for young people on earthworms—from their "wonderful, streamlined" adaptation to the environment to their "huge effect" on soil and essential role in decomposition. Although this is a non-fiction book, it is also listed in the Literature Connections for *Terrarium Habitats* as one of the most accessible and scientific books for young people on the earthworm.

Fast Plants/Bottle Biology. From the University of Wisconsin Department of Plant Pathology, these are hundreds of great activities you can do with 2-liter bottles. For more information, call (608) 263-5645, or write: Fast Plants/Bottle Biology, University of Wisconsin, Department of Plant Pathology, 1630 Linden Drive, Madison WI 53706.

Compost! Growing Gardens From Your Garbage by Linda Glaser, illustrated by Anca Hariton, is an excellent, colorful, and highly accessible book for the entire family published by The Millbrook Press, Brookfield, Connecticut, 1996. Another book by the same author, Wonderful Worms, *also connects well to* Terrarium Habitats.

From Food to Fertilizer by Charles C. Dahlberg, Young Scott Books, 1973. Diagrams the food chain for young readers.

Full Option Science System (FOSS), developed by the FOSS Project at the Lawrence Hall of Science, published by Encyclopaedia Britannica Educational Corporation, Chicago. A number of FOSS modules relate very well to the activities in Terrarium Habitats. These include, for Kindergarten—"Animals Two by Two," for Grades 1 and 2—both the "New Plants" and "Insects" modules, and for Grades 5 and 6—the "Environments" module. Several other modules relate to a deeper study of soil, such as "Pebbles, Sand, and Silt" for Grades 1 and 2, and "Earth Materials" for Grades 3 and 4.

Let It Rot! The Gardener's Guide to Composting by Stu Campbell, Storey Communications, Inc., Pownal, Vermont 05261, 1990.

Let's Talk Trash: The Kid's Book About Recycling by Kelly McQueen and David Fassler, M.D., with the Environmental Law Foundation, Waterfront Books, 1991.

Life Lab Science, a comprehensive curriculum for K–3 (based on the earlier activity guide The Growing Classroom: Garden-Based Science by Roberta Jaffe and Gary Appel) developed by Life Lab Science Program, Inc., 1156 High Street, Santa Cruz, CA 95064. (408) 459-2001. A nationally field-tested currriculum in life, earth, and the physical sciences which includes a teacher's resource book, videodisc, science discovery kit, garden reference book, garden log, lab books, and a "guess-test-tell" poster.

National Geographic, "Do We Treat Our Soil Like Dirt?" by Boyd Gibbons. Volume 166, Number 3, September 1984, National Geographic Society, Washington, D.C., 1984, pages 351–388. Outstanding article on erosion and the human impact on soil, with numerous related features, illustrations and photographs. A color map of the United States shows the soil groups that predominate by region; striking illustrations and close-up photographs show the denizens of the soil and explain their interconnections with it. A photo essay on the art of farming follows.

The Pillbug Project: A Guide to Investigation by Robin Burnett, with illustrations by Sergey Ivanov. Grades 3–7, 110 pages, 1992. Published by the National Science Teacher's Association, the Pillbug Project suggests exploratory and investigative activities that help develop observational skills and also focus on structure and behavior. Concepts of cooperative learning, a variety of assessment techniques, and pages that can be copied to form individual student logbooks are included. A story about the adventures of Patricia Pillbug is woven throughout the activities. This excellent resource is available for $16.50 from the NSTA, 1742 Connecticut Avenue NW, Washington, D.C. 20009-1171.

Snail by Jens Olesen, Silver Burdett Press, Simon & Shuster, New Jersey, 1986.

Snails by Hubert S. Zim and Lucretia Krantz, illustrated by René Martin, William Morrow and Company, New York, 1975.

Sunset's New Western Garden Book, Lane Publishing Company, 1979 (and other years). This is a classic reference for gardeners and gardening and contains excellent and useful information on soils.

Super Science Red magazine, the March 1991 issue, on soil, Volume 2, Number 6. Scholastic, Inc., New York, 1991 and Super Science Red Teacher, March 1991. Concise activities described for students about what soil is made of, how soils differ, what water does in soil, what soil is good for growing, and what wind does to soil. On the back cover, students find the "hidden soil helpers," including the organisms featured in *Terrarium Habitats*. The "Teacher" edition provides additional background, introduction and presentation suggestions, and ways to extend the activities.

Technology in the Curriculum: Science Resource Guide, produced for the California State Department of Education by the Lawrence Hall of Science, California State Department of Education, Sacramento, 1986. Pages 165–186 include the "Animal Homes Unit Plan" by Gigi Bridges, Kimi Hosoume, and Katharine Barrett, which provided the original impetus for this GEMS guide in the form of "Make a Forest Floor Terrarium." There are several other class sessions and also an "Animal Homes Computer Game" by Carol Turnbull, Tom Burke, and Gigi Bridges that appeared in the science diskette that was included in the Technology in the Curriculum package received by California schools at the time of publication. For information on current availability contact: Publication Sales, California State Department of Education, P.O. Box 271, Sacramento, CA 95802-0271.

Waste Education Clearinghouse Listing of Materials Available, Waste Education Clearinghouse, OWM, 1350 Energy Lane, St. Paul, MN 55108, 1-800-677-6300. A catalog of free waste education materials.

What's Under the Ground? by Susan Mayes, EDC Publishing, Tulsa, Oklahoma, 1989. Part of Starting Point Science Series (Ages 6–8).

The World Beneath Your Feet by Judith Rinard, National Geographic Society, 1985.

Worms Eat My Garbage by Mary Appelhof. Flower Press, Kalamazoo, Michigan, 49002, 1982. A complete and practical guide to worm composting.

BE SURE TO SEE THE LITERATURE CONNECTIONS LIST ON PAGE 79.

Dear Parents,

As you probably know, our class is assembling terrariums as part of a science project. The terrariums are homes for various plants and animals that typically live in or on the forest floor. Observing what happens in the terrariums gives students a chance to learn about the habitats and adaptations of animals that live in this type of environment as well as gain knowledge about the role these plants and animals play in the larger ecosystem.

We need your help in making this the best learning experience possible. Please consider collecting one or more of the following items and sending it to school with your child.

SMALL ANIMALS such as garden snails, slugs, beetles, garden crickets, garden spiders, millipedes, etc. Please do not collect poisonous spiders, centipedes, or flying animals such as adult butterflies, flies, moths, ladybugs, or the same animals in their younger life stages, like caterpillars. Also, thank you, but we don't want your ants!

PLANTS such as marigolds, ivy, sweet alyssum, violets, small ferns, and/or strawberry plants.

FOOD ITEMS such as potato, carrot, apple, corn on the cob, clean egg shells, lettuce, dried beans, etc. Please do not collect soft fruits, meats, candy, or vegetables that have a strong odor when the decompose like cabbage and broccoli.

INANIMATE NATURAL OBJECTS such as rocks, shells, sand, dried twigs, seeds, etc.

THANKS in advance for your efforts! And ask your child to tell you more about what we're doing!

Clay
Less than
1/12500 in.

Silt
Up to 1/500 in.

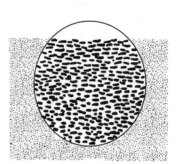

Clay

Fine sand
Up to 1/250 in.

Medium sand
Up to 1/50 in.

Sand

Largest sand
particles
1/12 in.

Loam

Behind the Scenes

This background section is intended to provide the teacher with additional information that may prove helpful in presenting these activities and in responding to student questions. It is not meant to be read out loud to students or duplicated for them to read.

The Living Soil

Soil is more than dirt! It is a mixture of mineral particles, air, water, and living and dead organisms. The soil layer that covers the earth contains millions of plants and animals. Living things interact with the non-living soil by creating tunnels for water and air, recycling nutrients, and mixing mineral particles throughout the soil. Organisms such as earthworms, isopods, bacteria, and fungi help to decompose dead plants and animals. Nutrients from the decomposing materials are left in the soil where they can be used by plants. The plants in turn provide food for animals and the cycle begins again.

Soils come in a variety of colors, textures, and odors. When wet, soils take on other characteristics: they become sticky, slick, slippery, and ready for squeezing and molding. Because young students may inadvertently inhale or eat soil, collect the soil from a garden area that has not been sprayed with chemicals or used by pets. Soils also can contain molds and fungi which cause allergies in some people.

The Soil Profile Test

The soil profile test is a simple test your students can conduct to observe the structure and texture of the soil. Soil structure determines how well a soil drains and retains water, air, heat, and nutrients. The size and shape of the mineral particles in soil determines the structure.

Clay particles are microscopic in size and are flat in shape. Due to their flatness, there are smaller spaces between them for air and for little amounts of water to drain. But clay particles hold water and contain important nutrients that are not removed by drainage. Clay soils are heavy, and tend to become compacted and hard for plant roots to penetrate. Students will characterize them as sticky or tacky, easy to roll into a ball, and very similar to modeling clay. When alum (aluminum ammonium sulfate) is added to the soil and water it physically binds to the clay assisting in the separation of the clay from the soil solution. Next, the differing weights of each mineral particle create the layers or profile observed in the vial. *Silt* is the next size particle. Each particle is larger than a clay particle and rounder in shape. Silt therefore drains better than clay and allows for larger air spaces for roots. *Sand* particles are the largest particles and are round in shape. Sandy soils provide good drainage, they warm quickly and have large spaces for air. Sandy soils also dry out quickly, provide few nutrients and often lose the nutrients present through drainage.

Clay
Less than
1/12500 in.

Silt
Up to1/500 in.

Fine Sand
Up to 1/250 in.

Medium Sand
Up to 1/50 in.

Largest Sand
Particles
1/12 in.

Loam soils have the characteristics of all three mineral particles. They contain about equal parts of clay, silt and sand. A loam soil is an ideal soil for terrariums and gardens. This soil should drain well without drying out too quickly. A loam should maintain enough air and water for healthy root growth. An important addition to a loam soil is *organic matter.* It is the decaying remains of once-living plants and animals. It is important because it improves aeration and drainage in heavy clay soils. In sandy soils, it helps to hold water and nutrients. The breakdown of organic matter releases nutrients to be used by plants. Ground bark, leaf mold, manure, and compost are different types of organic matter that can be added to garden soil. Do not use *potting soil* in your terrariums. The process used to produce potting soil leaves salts and other toxins that can harm ground-dwelling organisms.

An Introduction to the Terrarium

A terrarium is any enclosed container with soil that has been set up to house plants and small land animals. Glass or plastic tanks, storage boxes, deli salad containers, fish bowls, and bottles make good terrariums. It is best to have clear sides on your container to let in enough light, and to offer good viewing. A cover or lid with a few tiny holes is preferable to control the moisture level and air flow in the terrarium.

Maintaining Terrariums

Unlike most animal habitats, terrariums take very little maintenance! The main problems occur when terrariums are over-watered. Don't worry if the lush patch of grass turns yellow and begins to rot—this is part of the natural cycle of plants that will unfold as your students watch. Also, don't be surprised if a snail eats all foliage in sight! Providing enough supplementary food, adding more seeds and plants and/or removing one or more animals can stimulate new growth and new interactions to observe.

Place the terrariums in an area in the classroom that is light but does not get direct sunlight. The students can give the terrarium two squirts of water with the spray bottle once a week at most. Spray even less if the terrarium is smaller than a shoe box. The terrarium should always be slightly damp, but not soggy. The soil is better drier than too wet. If too much mold appears, let the terrarium dry out before watering again.

Encourage the following experiment: mist only one side or corner of the terrarium to create a moisture gradient. Which animals and plants seem to prefer the wetter side? the drier side? To keep the terrarium alive throughout the school year and the cycles cycling, students can periodically add small pieces of fruit, vegetables, egg shells, leaves, seeds, and new plants and animals.

The lid of the terrarium can be removed carefully to get a better look. If the terrarium is handled gently, the crawling and jumping insects will stay in the terrarium. Leaves, potatoes, cardboard tube, twigs can be carefully lifted or turned to observe the animals below. Items should be returned to their original positions after observing. Within a week, lifting the terrarium to look at the bottom may reveal plant roots, earthworm tunnels, or the animals themselves.

A terrarium kept in the classroom will do best when kept damp, cool, and in indirect sunlight. Here are some suggestions if problems do arise:

• **Too much mold:** if mold covers more than 1/8 the surface of the terrarium, remove the rotting material or leave the lid of the terrarium ajar to help dry it out. Some mold is fine; it is another interesting decomposer breaking down the organic material.

• **Too much moisture:** Wipe the inside of the lid and sides of the terrarium with a paper towel to remove excess moisture. Leave the lid of the terrarium ajar to help dry it out.

• **Too many small flies and gnats:** If there are small flying insects in a terrarium, it might be too wet, or there might be too much rotting food. These insects are not a problem in and of themselves, and can in fact provide another organism for your students to observe and discuss. If you want to get rid of them, then change the habitat so it no longer appeals, by making it less moist, and removing the moist food they are eating and breeding on.

• **No plants or sprouts:** If snails or other animals eat most of the foliage in a terrarium, add more seeds, plant more plants, add alternate food items, and/or reduce the number of animals in the terrarium. Some classes have decided to just have visits from the snails.

• **A dead-looking terrarium:** If you have tried all of the above suggestions, then perhaps your terrarium is too hot from leaving it in direct sunlight or near a heater. Constant temperatures of over 90 degrees will kill the animals. At cold temperatures (below 60 degrees) animals will slow down and burrow in the soil.

If you ever wish to dismantle the terrarium, have the students return the animals to an appropriate outdoor spot.

Adding Animals and Making Observations

Small animals such as pill bugs, sow bugs, earthworms, beetles, crickets, snails, or slugs can be collected safely by older students or by younger students with a supervising adult. Adding the animals to the terrarium is an exciting activity. Students of all ages watch carefully as the animals hide under a plant, eat a seed, or crawl under the paper tunnel. These activities help students overcome unnecessary fears of harmless animals and encourage gentleness and respect toward small creatures.

Some animals are not suitable for collecting or for living in the terrarium. Students should be warned about black widow and brown recluse spiders that have poisonous bites. Centipedes and garden spiders may bite so it is not recommended for younger students to collect them. Butterflies and moths do not do well in a terrarium because their natural food, nectar from flowers, is not available. Ants can escape from the small openings of the container. Ladybugs can be kept if aphids are provided for food.

Through their daily observations of the terrarium, the students see how the things they have added become shelter, water, or food for the animals. Most students respond to the changes that they see take place: plants and roots grow, leaves are eaten, seeds sprout, small animals multiply! Working together to build and care for the terrarium encourages team cooperation and responsibility.

Earthworms

The small pinkish-red earthworms commonly found in gardens are called redworms. Bait stores sell them for fishing, too. Their Latin name is *Eisenia foetida*. Earthworms belong to the group of invertebrates called annelids meaning "ringed or segmented." The large, 5–6 inch long earthworms are called nightcrawlers because of their nocturnal habits. Go out into your yard after dark with a flashlight and you will see them crawling on top of the ground in search of dried leaves to eat.

One way to get earthworms is to dig them up with a trowel or shovel. You may end up slicing one in half and if this happens, you will have two halves of a dead worm! Earthworms can regenerate the tips of their head and tail *only* if they are cut before the first twelve segments or after the last five.

There is another way for a whole class to collect earthworms from a school lawn without damaging the worms. Get an adult-size shovel and pick a day about a week after a rainstorm so the lawn soil is wet but not soaking. Insert the whole head of the shovel into the ground so it can stand straight up without holding it. Pull the handle back and let go quickly so that the shovel and the handle "twang" like a plucked guitar string. Continue to "twang" the shovel. The quick movement of the shovel is sending vibrations into the ground. Earthworms are very sensitive to vibrations. Their response is to move upward to the surface, perhaps as a defense from a hungry mole searching for an earthworm meal. Your students, who are spread out around the shovel, can collect the worms as they appear on the surface of the lawn! One teacher has suggested that you don't even need the vibrating shovel. Have your students jump or stomp on the ground and the worms will respond by coming to the surface.

Earthworm Anatomy

Earthworms have a digestive tract that runs the length of their body. Food is ground up by small stones in the gizzard and then passed on to the intestine. Enzymes in the intestine breakdown the food and nutrients. Oxygen, absorbed through the moisture on the skin, and nutrients and wastes, are carried by two main blood vessels. Earthworm blood contains hemoglobin like human blood, thus the red color. Five pairs of hearts situated at the front of the worm pump the blood. The hearts are thick blood vessels that connect the dorsal and ventral blood vessels. Students should be able to see the blood vessels, the hearts, the pumping blood, and the intestine by holding a lightly pigmented worm up to a light. (Place the worm in a clear cup first.) Externally, worms are segmented and have bristles or *setae* on each segment. Use nightcrawlers to observe earthworm segments and setae. Worms have no eyes or ears, but their pointed head and round body is sensitive to vibrations and chemicals. Earthworms absorb water and oxygen from their skin. Remind the students to keep an earthworm moist at all times when observing it or it can dry out and die.

Earthworms prefer to eat dried leaves and other organic matter, but will eat soil and extract the decomposing nutrients if nothing else is available. Chemicals in the digestive tract change nutrients into a usable form for the worm. A worm's waste or castings contain nutrients that enrich the soil and provide the necessary food for plant growth. An earthworm's tunneling also mixes and aerates the soil. Earthworms can move rocks and dirt **fifty times their own weight.** The humus layer on top of the soil contains the richest layer of decomposing material. Earthworms mix the humus into lower layers during their nighttime movements. Worms are even known to pull whole leaves down into their burrows. Encourage students to make note of the positions of the leaves in the terrarium. The next morning look for moved or missing leaves!

Earthworm Reproduction

Another structure easily seen on nightcrawlers and sometimes seen on redworms is the clitellum. It is the light colored band around the middle of the worm. The clitellum secretes a mucus that will form over the egg case.

Earthworms are hermaphroditic. They produce both eggs and sperm, but must be fertilized by another worm to produce fertile eggs. Worms mate by lining up next to each in opposite directions and then, fertilizing each other. A mucus film forms around the clitellum and slips down toward the tail. As the egg case is released, the mucous film covers the case and protects the case in the soil. Egg cases are the size of a grain of rice and are oval in shape. They are usually dark in color. Only a few worms will hatch out of an egg case. Young worms are tiny and very light in color, but otherwise look and move like adult earthworms.

Isopods

Terrestrial isopods are commonly known as pillbugs and sowbugs. They belong to a group of crustaceans that have a tough segmented outer shell and seven pairs of identical jointed walking legs (Iso=equal, Pod=legs). Sowbugs and pillbugs are also referred to as wood lice and pill wood lice. They are found in all tropical and temperate parts of the world.

Isopods are scavengers and decomposers, eating dead plants and animals, and living things, too. Their waste, called frasse, comes in an unusual cubic shape. As with all decomposers, the nutrients in their waste contributes to the richness of the soil. Isopods are usually nocturnal, hiding during the day in damp dark places to avoid the heat and light. All isopods need moisture and without it, will die in two hours. They have special sense organs on their outer skin that detect moisture. As isopods grow, their skin will shed or molt. You may see the molt immediately after it comes off, but soon the isopod will eat it for nourishment. All isopods are harmless, and easy to pick up and examine. Although looking very similar, pillbugs and sowbugs are separate species, with other subspecies, too.

Sowbugs

Sowbug

Sowbugs have a flat body with fringed edges. They are usually dark bluish-grey in color and have two distinctive spines protruding out the rear. Sowbugs have two jointed antennae on the head end as well. To avoid moisture loss, sowbugs congregate together under damp wood or garden pots. Out in the open they move very quickly, a good defense against predator spiders and birds. Sowbugs also secrete a bad-tasting liquid to repel themselves from ants, spiders and centipedes. Their dark color blends in with the surroundings. Unlike pillbugs, sowbugs cannot roll into a ball.

Sowbug reproduction has been observed, but little is known about pillbug breeding habits. After a female sowbug is fertilized by a male, a triangular-shaped pouch appears between her forelegs. Twenty or more legs are laid, and carried in the pouch for six weeks. The pouch is translucent and enlarged, so you can see the eggs and the young that emerge from the eggs with a hand lens. When they come out of the pouch slit they are very light in color and have two dark eyes like their parents. It is very easy to rear sowbugs in your terrarium.

Pillbugs

Pillbugs are also called rolly-pollys by children. They are very dark grey and have a domed-shaped body with no fringe. They have two antennae in the front but none in the rear. Their distinctive behavior is rolling into a ball when startled. This behavior protects their fleshy underside from predators and from the loss of water. The dark color and ball shape help to camouflage them on the ground. Pillbugs are less susceptible to drying out than sowbugs. Because of this, they are more likely to be seen walking on the surface of the ground during the day. Pillbugs prefer a drier habitat than sowbugs, so provide a dry spot in your terrarium for them.

Pillbug

Crickets

Crickets live well in a dry or slightly damp terrarium. They are active, eat a variety of foods, and the adult males make nice chirping sounds by rubbing two wings together. Most pet stores sell crickets very inexpensively as live food for reptiles and amphibians.

Cricket Homes, Reproduction, and Food

Crickets will seek out dark, dry places in the terrarium. Dry leaves and paper tubes make excellent cricket hiding places. If you have an egg-laying female, she may extend her ovipositor or egg tube under the surface of the moist soil and deposit her eggs. The eggs hatch in three weeks. The young crickets look like tiny wingless versions of the adults.

Along with the dried leaves, seeds, and plants, the crickets will eat pieces of potato, apple, and carrot. Juicy fruits and vegetables will provide the water they need. Grains, bran meal, oatmeal, or dried dog food are other foods that crickets eat.

Cricket Handling

Crickets are difficult to touch or pet because they are so active. But with adult supervision young students can gently scoop one into a hand and carefully curl the fingers around it to form a cage. Crickets do not bite or sting, but they do tickle!

Garden Snails and Slugs

Garden snails and slugs are two other animals that do well in a terrarium. In temperate climates, they are easily found in moist, dark areas of a garden and are safely handled by students.

Snails and slugs belong to a large group of animals called mollusks. They have no bones inside of their fleshy bodies. The snail produces a shell over its body. The shell, attached to its soft body part, grows as the snail grows. The shell acts as a hard covering to protect the snail from abrasion and from drying out. A slug does not have a shell but secretes a layer of mucus that also keeps it from losing moisture. Snails and slugs are hermaphroditic. Like earthworms, they must be fertilized by another to produce fertile eggs. Snail eggs are light in color, translucent, and the size of small peas. Only one snail or slug will hatch from one egg. A common myth is that snails can walk away from their shell and become a slug. A snail is permanently attached to its shell. Although related, snails and slugs are two different kinds of animals.

Snails and slugs move along surfaces with their "foot," which is covered with mucus to help them push across rough surfaces. When dried, this "slime" leaves the distinctive silvery trail of a snail's or slug's nightly movements. This trail is an easy way to map a snails movements in the terrarium or in a garden.

Snail and Slug Observations and Feeding

Coax a snail to extend its head and foot by misting it with water. Be patient, and watch for the slow uncurling of its head. Place the snail on its back (shell side down) and blow lightly across the foot to stimulate it to emerge. Look for the two eyes at the tip of the upper two feelers or tentacles. When touched gently, the eyes immediately retract into the tentacles. The lower two feelers are used as probes and move rhythmically when the snail moves forward. The tips of the lower tentacles contain the sense organs that detect odors.

Offer a piece of lettuce to a snail. Watch the dark, fingernail-shaped mouth gnaw at the lettuce. The mouth, or radula, acts like sandpaper grinding away at fruits, vegetables, leaves, and grain. Snails and slugs also eat other decaying matter. Place only one small snail or slug in the terrarium so they will not eat up all the plants and sprouts.

Holding Snails and Slugs

Students enjoy having snails and slugs crawl across their fingers and hands. These animals do not bite and are easily picked up. Slugs are very very sticky! Snail and slug slime can be washed off hands with water and a little soap. Avoid touching slugs and snails after using soaps or lotions. These products are immediately absorbed into the moist body tissue of the snails and slugs, and can harm them.

Summary Outlines

Activity 1: Exploring Soil

Getting Ready
A Week Before the Activity

1. Collect clean garden soil.

2. Mist soil and divide into plastic bags for each group.

3. Gather the rest of the materials needed for this activity.

4. Read "Behind the Scenes" information on soil.

The Day of the Activity

Set up two materials distribution stations and organize the materials into groups for each team.

Immediately Before the Activity

Cover the tables with newspapers.

Introducing the Activity

1. Introduce idea of soil. Brainstorm two lists on board: "Where have you found soil?" "What do you think we will find in the soils?"

2. Explain that they will be using four of their five senses to make observations about soil.

3. After getting their materials, tell students that they will each carefully observe a spoonful of soil and write or draw descriptions about the soil. It's okay to discuss with others.

Investigating the Soil

1. Have one student from each group come and get materials.

2. Circulate among teams to encourage their investigations.

3. Help younger students articulate what they see; challenge older students to make more observations.

4. Encourage students to share ideas with each other.

Reflecting: Soil is More than Dirt!

1. Have students share and discuss their findings. Compare with their list of predictions. Ask, "What was something unexpected that you found about your soil?"

2. Have your students help you draw a simple food chain on the board, depicting the relationship between soil, plants, animals, and humans.

3. Discuss the critical role soil plays for human survival.

4. For older students, discuss global problem of soil destruction.

5. Have students return soil to bags. Clean up and have students wash hands.

Activity 2: Building a Terrarium Habitat

Getting Ready
Several Days Before the Activity

1. Read *"Behind the Scenes"* information pertaining to the handling and maintaining of soil, plants, and animals.

2. Gather the materials needed to present the activity.

3. Use a push pin to punch 6-10 holes in the lids of the terrarium containers.

The Day of the Activity

1. Set up two materials distribution stations and organize the materials into groups for each team.

2. Mist soil if it is dry.

Immediately Before the Activity

Cover tables with newspapers.

What's In A Terrarium?

1. Ask, "What might you find on the forest floor?" Show how you have gathered some of these things so they may put them in a container (terrarium) to make a home for living things.

2. Demonstrate the making of a terrarium or just explain the various components verbally step-by-step. (Note: the following student choices can be limited depending on the situation and the teacher's preferences.)

- Adding soil: a) how much; b) its composition; c) the landscape of the soil.

- Planting plants: a) where they plant their plant; b) how many plants; and c) where.

- Spreading seeds: a) what kind(s) of seeds to plant; b) how much; and (c) where.

- Adding litter (twigs, bark, and leaves): a) whether to add leaves and twigs; b) how much to add; and c) where to put them.

- Adding moisture: LIMIT THE NUMBER OF SQUIRTS TO FOUR PER STUDENT; two as they begin building the terrarium and two when it's complete.

3. If you plan to provide roles for the students, assign them now.

4. Have teams plan their terrariums before distributing materials.

Building the Terrariums

1. Have representatives from each team gather materials from the distribution station.

2. Circulate among the teams. Encourage cooperation and MISTING LIGHTLY.

3. Give students a chance to see each other's terrariums.

Introducing the Concept of Habitat

1. Define the concept of a habitat [a place where animals live, like a neighborhood]. Discuss what a habitat needs to provide [food, shelter, moisture, light, protection].

2. Ask, "What kinds of animals might live in this habitat?" Tell students they will be adding animals to their terrariums in future sessions.

Caring for and Observing the Terrariums over Time

1. Ask, "What kinds of changes will we see in our terrariums?" Discuss procedures for terrarium maintenance:

   a. Decide on a place where the terrarium will be kept.
   b. Decide on a schedule for watering.
   c. Lids stay on terrariums.
   d. Terrariums should not be bumped or shaken.

2. Plan a routine for observing the terrariums and keeping a record of changes.

Providing a Dark Place in the Habitat

1. Ask teams to write their names, and the name of their terrarium, on the black papers with a labels. Demonstrate how to attach this flap to the side of each terrarium.

2. Have students attach the label flap, move terrariums to their spots, clean up, and wash their hands.

Activity 3: Adding Earthworms to the Terrarium

Getting Ready
A Week Before the Day of the Activity

1. Read "Behind the Scenes" information on earthworms.

2. Collect earthworms and store in a cool, moist place.

3. Duplicate student sheets.

4. Gather the rest of the materials needed for the activity.

5. Make a milk carton tray for each pair of students.

The Day of the Activity

Set up two materials distribution stations and organize the materials into groups for each team.

Immediately Before the Activity

1. Place one worm in a cup for each students. Mist and cover.

2. Have terrariums nearby but not in the team work areas.

Observing Earthworms!

1. Tell your students that today they will put some living animals into their terrariums. Have them guess what lives underground and then reveal that they will be working with earthworms.

2. Ask, "What do you know about earthworms? Where do you see them? What were they doing?" Allow students to discuss their experiences with earthworms.

3. If students are negative, use this as an opportunity to say that they will be learning what is positive and interesting about worms. They don't have to touch the worms. They do need to be gentle with the worms.

4. Demonstrate how to observe the structure of earthworms. Invite them to record what structures they observe on the student sheet or in their journals.

5. Demonstrate how they can observe the behavior of earthworms.

6. Have one person from each team get materials.

7. Circulate among the teams to help them with their observations and recording. Mist worms as needed. Encourage gentle, quiet handling.

8. Focus and challenge students to find the head, the tail, internal structures, and to determine specific reactions to various stimuli, such as touch, light, dark, moisture, dryness.

9. Encourage them to record what structures and behaviors they observe.

What Did You Find Out?

1. Ask students to place worms back in cups.

2. Have a team member return equipment while you draw a large outline of an earthworm on the board.

3. Lead a discussion about earthworm observations. List students' observations on the board. Add structures or labels to the worm outline as appropriate.

4. As students bring up earthworm characteristics, ask students to speculate on the benefit of the structures or behaviors they noticed to the survival of the worm in an underground home.

5. Introduce the concept of adaptation [structures or behaviors that help an animal to survive in it's environment].

6. Tell how earthworms' adaptations benefit the soil and in turn, plants

that grow in the soil. Explain how earthworms are recyclers. Introduce the word decomposition. For older students, name this as the nutrient cycle.

Adding Earthworms to the Terrariums

1. Have student predict what the earthworm will do when placed inside the terrarium.

2. Have the original terrarium team get together and send a team member to bring the terrarium to the table. Invite students to put their earthworms in the terrarium, one at a time, and observe their behavior.

3. Have each team clean up and wash their hands.

Activity 4: Adding Isopods to the Terrarium

Getting Ready
A Week Before the Activity

1. Read "**Behind the Scenes**" information on isopods.

2. Collect pillbugs and sowbugs and store in a cool, moist place.

3. Duplicate one student sheet for each student.

4. Gather the rest of the materials needed for the activity.

5. Make a milk carton tray for each pair of students (or reuse the trays you used in the Earthworms session).

The Day of the Activity

Set up two materials distribution stations and organize the materials into groups for each team.

Immediately Before the Activity

1. Place two pill bugs and two sowbugs into a cup for each student. Mist and cover.

2. Have terrariums nearby but not in the team work areas.

Observing Isopods!

1. Tell your students that they will be observing another living animal and putting it in their terrariums. Have them guess what lives under leaves or logs on the ground and then reveal that they will be working with isopods.

2. Share the more common names for isopods. Ask, "What do you know about isopods? Where do you see them? What were they doing?" Allow students to discuss their experiences with earthworms.

3. If students are negative, use this as an opportunity to say that they will be learning what is positive and interesting about isopods. They don't have to touch the isopods. They do need to be gentle with the isopods.

4. Demonstrate how to observe the structure of isopods. Invite them to record what structures they observe on the student sheet or in their journals.

5. Demonstrate how they can observe the behavior of isopods.

6. Have one person from each team get materials.

7. Circulate among the teams to help them with their observations and recording. Mist isopods as needed. Encourage gentle, quiet handling.

8. Focus and challenge students to find the antennae, head, eyes, number of legs, segments, and to determine specific reactions to various stimuli, such as touch, light, dark, moisture, dryness.

9. Encourage them to record what structures and behaviors they observe.

What Did You Find Out?

1. Ask students to place isopods back in cups.

2. Lead a discussion about isopod observations. List students' observations on the board. Invite volunteers to draw and label a picture of an isopod on the board as appropriate.

3. Ask questions to bring out the different characteristics of isopods, both physical and behavioral. Do not tell them they have two kinds of isopods, rather, let them discover this through their discussion and observations.

4. If students have not discovered that there are two different kinds of isopods, then ask, "Are all of the isopods the same?"

5. Go through the list of observations listed on the board and have students pick out the characteristics that belong to the ones that roll into a ball. Identify these as "pillbugs." Do the same for the "other" type of isopod. Identify these as "sowbugs."

6. As students bring up isopod characteristics, ask students to speculate on the benefit of the structures or behaviors they noticed to the survival of isopods in a ground home. List their ideas in a separate column next to the list of characteristics.

7. Review the concept of adaptation [structures or behaviors that help an animal to survive in it's environment].

8. Compare the adaptations for defense of the pillbug and sowbug.

9. Tell how isopods' adaptations benefit the soil and in turn, plants that grow in the soil. Explain that like earthworms, isopods are recyclers and decomposers. Re-emphasize the importance of decomposition in the ecosystem of a forest floor (and everywhere!).

Adding Isopods to the Terrariums

1. Have students predict what the isopods will do when placed inside the terrarium.

2. Have the original terrarium team get together and send a team member to bring the terrarium to the table. Invite students to put their isopods, leaves, potato chunk, and cardboard roll in the terrarium, one at a time, and observe what the isopods do.

3. Have each team clean up and wash their hands.

Activity 5: Adding More to the Terrarium

Getting Ready

1. Read the information on page 43 about what to add, and on snail and cricket observations (pages 46,47) and on other animals in "Behind the Scenes." Decide what you'd like your students to add to their terrariums.

2. Decide how you will gather additional things to add to the terrarium and go ahead and begin collecting.

3. Decide how you want to structure the activity of adding more items to the terrariums.

4. As desired, prepare or have students create observation sheets for the organisms to be added. Consider assigning journal or other writing activities.

Interactions Abound

1. Explain that students will be adding other organisms/materials to their terrariums.

2. If snails are being added, conduct activities described under **"Snail Observations."**

3. If crickets are being added, have students do activities described under **"Cricket Observations."**

4. Encourage students to record findings, ask questions, test assumptions, and learn more about their "world in a box."

Assessment Suggestions

Selected Student Outcomes

1. Students articulate that an animal's habitat provides air, water, food, and shelter.

2. Students understand the concept of adaptation and are able to describe the structures and behaviors of an animal that help it survive in its habitat.

3. Students can explain how small animals that live in the soil help break down plant and animal material to return the nutrients to the soil.

4. Students improve their ability to make careful observations.

5. Students are able to identify changes that occur in the terrarium and can determine when those changes are part of a larger cycle.

Built-In Assessment Activities

A Terrarium Habitat

In Activity 2, teams of students design and build a habitat for small animals that live in or on the soil. During the project, the teacher can ask each team to explain why they add soil, water, plants, seeds, and bark. If students have terrarium journals, they can describe how their habitat provides water, air, shelter, and food for small animals. (Outcome 1)

Animals in the Terrarium

In Activities 3–5, students observe earthworms, pillbugs, sow bugs, and snails. They note physical characteristics and behaviors that will help the animals survive in the terrarium. Over many weeks, the students observe how the animals behave in their new habitat. As students study the animals, the teacher can pose questions that will reveal students' observation skills and their developing knowledge about animal behavior. For example, the teacher can ask students how an earthworm's shape and movements help it burrow in the soil. Students can write down these ideas in their journal and later add behaviors they observe to support their ideas. The teacher can review journal entries or have students share their observations with the whole class. (Outcomes 1, 2, 4, 5)

Assessment Suggestions (continued)

Decomposers

As students continue to observe the changes in their terrarium, they will begin to understand how small creatures help to recycle nutrients in the habitat. The students observe how animals eat leaves, seeds and other plant material. Even a dead cricket will "disappear" in the terrarium! Students observe waste left by the animal and a build up of soil. The teacher can ask students to explain the relationship between these events in their journal or during a class discussion. (Outcomes 3, 4, 5)

Additional Assessment Ideas

An Isopod's Journal

Have students imagine they are a pill bug or sow bug that lives in a terrarium. Ask them to them to write about what they would experience in one day of their life. (Outcomes 1, 3, 4, 5) **This activity is featured as a Case Study on page 35 of the GEMS assessment handbook,** *Insights and Outcomes: Assessments for Great Explorations in Math and Science.*

More Animals in the Terrarium

Invite students to bring in other small creatures to add to the habitat. Have them explain why they think the animals will survive in the terrarium. Challenge them to keep their terrarium animals alive through the school year and to continue to record observations and ideas in their journal. (Outcomes 1, 3, 4, 5)

Literature Connections

There are many great literature connections for *Terrarium Habitats.* Some of the books listed below focus on snails, crickets, ants, or salamanders that could live in a terrarium or on a forest floor. Interdependence, life cycle, and scale are emphasized through fantasy stories that ask the reader to view life from an animal's perspective. Other books look at the system of plants and animals that is nurtured by a decomposing tree. Also included are several inviting resource books or almanacs that give ideas for other fun, hands-on investigations of nature. See the Resources list on page 51 for some other non-fiction books.

You may also want to refer to the GEMS literature handbook: *Once Upon A GEMS Guide: Connecting Young People's Literature to Great Explorations in Math and Science* under other related GEMS guides, such as *Animals in Action, Earthworms, Mapping Animal Movements,* as well as under appropriate science themes and mathematics strands. We welcome your suggestions for literature connections and will consider them when this guide and the GEMS literature handbook are revised.

Chipmunk Song
by Joanne Ryder; illustrated by Lynne Cherry
E.P. Dutton, New York. 1987
Grades: K–5
A chipmunk goes about its activities in late summer, prepares for winter, and settles in until spring. The reader is put in the place of a chipmunk and participates in food gathering, hiding from predators, hibernating, and more. Roots, tunnels, stashes of acorns and other facets of the imagined environment loom large and lifelike.

Deep Down Underground
by Olivier Dunrea
Macmillan, New York. 1989
Grades: Preschool–3
Cumulative counting book led off by "one wee moudiewort" (Scottish word for type of mole) and a creepy cadre of earthworms, caterpillars, beetles, toads and spiders, sowbugs, garter snakes, and red ants. The dynamic language makes it great for reading aloud individually or in a group wriggling, wrangling, scooching, and scraping.

Earthworm
by Adrienne Souter-Perrot; illustrated by Etienne Delessent
Creative Editions, Mankato, Minnesota, 1993
Grades: Preschool-2
Simply and accurately written, and elegantly illustrated, this is an excellent early childhood introduction to earthworms and their revitalization of the soil.

Earthworms, Dirt, and Rotten Leaves
by Molly McLaughlin
Avon, New York. 1990
Grades: 4–7
The earthworm and its environment are explored and suggestions made for experiments to examine the survival of the earthworm in its habitat. Answers the question, "Why would anyone want to have anything to do with earthworms?" Recipient of awards for writing from Library of Congress, American Library Association, and New York Academy of Sciences.

The Empty Lot
by Dale H. Fife; illustrated by Jim Arnosky
Sierra Club Books/Little, Brown Co., Boston. 1991
Grades: 2–4
What good is a vacant lot? City-dweller Harry Hale owns one, but when he goes to take a good look before selling it, he is amazed to find that the lot is far from empty. It's pulsing with life: birds and their nests; ants, beetles, fungi, and molds in the soil; and frogs and dragonflies near the stream. He is so impressed by the utilization of the different habitat areas that he changes his for sale sign to read "occupied lot—every square inch in use."

The Fall of Freddie the Leaf
by Leo Buscaglia, Ph.D.
Charles B. Slack, Inc./Holt, Rinehart and Winston, New York, 1982
Grades: All ages
This simply-told story, with beautiful color photographs and a real leaf on the inside back cover, describes the growth, maturity, decay, and death of a leaf named Freddie and his friends and is "dedicated to all children who have even suffered a permanent loss, and to the grownups who could not find a way to explain it." Because the story is about leaves, it is also a good connection to what students learn in *Terrarium Habitats* about decomposition.

The Frog Alphabet Book
by Jerry Pallotta; illustrated by Ralph Masiello
Charlesbridge Publishing, Watertown, Mass. 1990
Grades: K–3
A beautifully illustrated book that shows the diversity of frogs and other "awesome amphibians" from around the world.

Frogs, Toads, Lizards, and Salamanders
by Nancy W. Parker and Joan R. Wright; illustrated by Nancy W. Parker.
Greenwillow, New York. 1990
Grades: 3–6
Physical characteristics, habits, and environment of 16 creatures are
encapsulated in rhyming couplets, text, and anatomical drawings, plus
glossaries, range maps, and a scientific classification chart. A great deal
of information is presented, the rhymes are engaging and humorous, and
the visual presentation terrific. "A slimy Two-toed Amphiuma terrified
Grant's aunt from Yuma" (she was picking flowers from a drainage
ditch).

The Girl Who Loved Caterpillars
adapted by Jean Merrill; illustrated by Floyd Cooper
Philomel Books/Putnam & Grosset, New York. 1992
Grades: 2–6
Based on a twelfth century Japanese story, this book is a wonderful and
early portrait of a highly independent and free-spirited girl, Izumi, who
loves caterpillars. Izumi wonders "Why do people make such a fuss
about butterflies and pay no attention to the creatures from which
butterflies come? It is caterpillars that are really interesting!" Izumi is
interested in the "original nature of things," and in doing things
naturally. Clever poetry is interspersed as part of the plot. Great
connection to the observation activities in *Terrarium Habitats*. An excellent
and relevant portrayal of an independent-thinking female role model.

Joyful Noise: Poems for Two Voices
by Paul Fleischman; illustrated by Eric Beddows
Harper & Row, New York. 1988
Grades: K–Adult
Fantastic series of poems celebrating insects that are meant to be read
aloud by two readers at once, sometimes merging into a duet. It includes
beetles and crickets, and many others, such as grasshoppers and cicadas.
The combination of rich scientific detail with poetry, humor, and a sense
of the ironic contrasts and division of labor in the lives and life changes
of insects is powerful and very involving. Students in upper level classes
might love performing these for the class. Newbery award winner.

Linnea's Almanac
by Christina Bjork; illustrated by Lena Anderson
R&S Books/Farrar, Straus & Giroux, New York. 1989
Grades: 3–6
Linnea keeps an almanac tracking her indoor and outdoor investigations
of nature over a year's time. She opens a bird restaurant in January and
goes beachcombing in July. The almanac is written in journal form with
simple monthly activities for young readers to do at home.

Linnea's Windowsill Garden

by Christina Bjork; illustrated by Lena Anderson

R&S Books/Farrar, Straus & Giroux, New York. 1988

Grades: 3–6

Linnea tells about her indoor garden. From seeds to cuttings to potted plants, Linnea describes the care of her plants throughout their life cycle. The friendly narration and simple information invites readers to try the activities and games at home.

The Magic School Bus Inside the Earth

by Joanna Cole

Scholastic, New York, 1987

Grades 3–6

Another in this highly educational and amusing series, as Ms. Frizzle takes her class on a field trip to the center of the Earth and back again. Much geological information is interspersed throughout. This book could serve as a good extension to the soil activities in *Terrarium Habitats*.

Nicky the Nature Detective

by Ulf Svedberg

R&S Books/Farrar, Straus & Giroux, New York. 1988

Grades: 3–8

Nicky loves to explore changes in nature. She watches a red maple tree and all the creatures and plants that live on or near the tree throughout the seasons. Her discoveries lead her to look carefully at the structure of the nesting place, why birds migrate, who left tracks in the snow, where butterflies go in the winter, and many more things. This book is packed with information and inviting graphic elements.

An Oak Tree Dies and a Journey Begins

by Louanne Norris and Howard E. Smith, Jr.; illustrated by Allen Davis

Crown, New York. 1979

Out of print

Grades: 3–5

An old oak tree on the bank of a river is uprooted by a storm and its journey to the sea begins. Animals seek shelter in the log, children fish from it, mussels attach to its side. A story of how a tree, even after it dies, contributes to the environment. Students will appreciate the fine pen and ink drawings.

Once There Was a Tree

by Natalia Romanova; illustrations by Gennady Spirin

Dial Books, Penguin, New York. 1983

Grades: K–6

A tree is struck by lightning, cut down, and left as a stump. A bark beetle lays her eggs under its bark, its larvae gnaw tunnels. Ants make their home there. A bear uses the stump to sharpen her claws. The stump is visited by birds, frogs, earwigs, and humans. It endures the weather. As a new tree grows from the stump, a question remains: "Whose tree is it?"

One Day in the Woods
by Jean C. George; illustrated by Gary Allen
Thomas Y. Crowell, New York. 1988
Grades: 4–7
On a day-long outing in a woodland forest, Rebecca, a "pony tailed explorer," searches for the elusive ovenbird. Her observation of, and interaction with, the plant and animal life are enhanced by realistic black and white drawings.

The Salamander Room
by Anne Mazer; illustrated by Steve Johnson
Alfred A. Knopf, New York. 1991
Grades: K–3
A little boy finds an orange salamander in the woods and thinks of the many things he can do to turn his room into a perfect salamander home. In the process, the habitat requirements of a forest floor dweller are nicely described.

The Snail's Spell
by Joanne Ryder; illustrated by Lynne Cherry
Puffin Books, New York. 1988
Grades: K–5
Imagine how it feels to be a snail and in the process learn something about the anatomy and locomotion of a snail. Though the picture-book format has a primary-level feel to the book, imagining you are a snail is interesting for older students as well. Outstanding Science Book for Young Children Award from the New York Academy of Sciences.

The Song in the Walnut Grove
by David Kherdian; illustrated by Paul O. Zelinsky
Alfred A. Knopf, New York. 1982
Grades: 4–6
A curious cricket named Ben meets Charley the grasshopper. Together they learn of each other's daytime and nighttime habits while living in a herb garden. The friendship between Ben and Charley grows when Ben rescues Charley from being buried in a pail of grain and they learn to appreciate each other's differences. This story weaves very accurate accounts of insect behavior with their contributions to the ecology of Walnut Grove.

Two Bad Ants
by Chris Van Allsburg
Houghton Mifflin and Co., Boston. 1988
Grades: Preschool–4
When two curious ants set off in search of beautiful sparkling crystals (sugar), it becomes a dangerous adventure that convinces them to return to the former safety of their ant colony. Illustrations are drawn from an ant's perspective, showing them lugging individual sugar crystals and other views from "the small."

When the Woods Hum
by Joanne Ryder; illustrated by Catherine Stock
William Morrow, New York. 1991
Grades: 1–4
Young Jenny, who has heard her father reminisce about the wonder of
hearing the woods hum, investigates periodical cicadas—"hummers."
They observe the wingless creepers emerging from underground, the
adult cicadas shedding their old skins, and the female laying eggs. A
page of sketches at the end of the book gives some detail, differentiating
between the annual and periodical cicada. The cycle motif is reinforced
when the grown-up Jenny and her father take her son to the woods so he
can hear the humming.

Whisper from the Woods
by Victoria Wirth, illustrated by A. Scott Banfill
Green Tiger Press (Simon & Shuster), New York, 1991.
Grades: Preschool–4
This stunningly designed book brings the woods alive with gorgeous
full-page color illustrations and poetic text that depict in detail trees,
vegetation, the seasons, and the animal life of the forest. The illustrations
blend in a tiny face within a seed that grows and grows to becomes a
mature tree within a forest of trees, all with human faces and with arms
and hands for roots that intertwine under the ground. In the summer,
"these trees, young and old, would lean together and whisper; sharing
thoughts and passing the wisdom of many years." The visual effects are
powerful and beautiful, conveying in a unique way the connection
between all living things and illustrating the life cycle. The purple cloth
cover, striking illustrations, and emotional impact make this book a true
treasure.

Wonderful Worms
by Linda Glaser; illustrated by Loretta Krupinski
The Millbrooke Press, Brookfield, Connecticut, 1992
Grades: Preschool-3
This is an excellent and unique, cleverly illustrated introduction to
earthworms and their work. The writing is particularly noteworthy for
its view from the child's perspective–"Worms feel sounds with their
whole bodies. They feel thunder when I walk."

Observing Earthworms

1. Draw what your earthworm looks like:

Inside View:

Outside View:

2. What does your earthworm do?

Name_____

Observing Isopods

1. Draw what your isopods look like:

Side View:

Top View:

Bottom View:

2. What do your isopods do?

Name_____

Observing Earthworms

1. Draw what your earthworm looks like:

Inside View:

Outside View:

2. What does your earthworm do?

Name_____

Observing Isopods

1. Draw what your isopods look like:

Side View:

Top View:

Bottom View:

2. What do your isopods do?